THE BOOK OF CRINGE

A collection of reasonably clean
but silly schoolboy jokes

By

Julian Walker

www.julianwalker.info

Grosvenor House
Publishing Limited

This book is published by
Grosvenor House Publishing Ltd
28-30 High Street, Guildford, Surrey, GU1 3EL.
www.grosvenorhousepublishing.co.uk

A CIP record for this book
is available from the British Library

ISBN 978-1-78148-920-8

To godchildren, nephews and nieces everywhere,
especially:

Amelia, Annie, Archie,
Emma, Ella-Blue, Finnbhar,
Fred, Harry, James (D), James (G),
Jess (B-G), Jess (H), Lucie,
Millie, Olivia, Peter,
Rebecca, Robin, Sebastian,
Tom and Will.

And in memory of Tim,
whose infectious laughter will always ring
long and loud in our memories.

Also by the author

The Cape Crusaders

In 1987, seven people embarked on a three month charity expedition to drive an old red Dennis fire engine from the northern tip of Europe to the southernmost point of Africa.

After almost five months, 37,000km, 21 countries, and a journey through rainforest, bush veldt, deserts and urban developments, the author was one of five who completed their odyssey.

The Cape Crusaders is his engaging account of the at times hazardous trip, including being mugged, arrested, having two near fatal accidents and a severe case of cerebral malaria. A must for any armchair adventure traveller.

What people have said about The Cape Crusaders:

"Heart-warming and laugh-out loud adventure story."

"Inspirational, insightful - and fun."

"Exquisitely English humour along a fascinating transcontinental adventure."

"Inspiring and real."

"Great adventurous read."

"Fun & funny."

www.thecapecrusaders.com

Over the years, my ability to remember and spout silly jokes has often lightened the mood and assisted with many a speechwriting session. It has certainly provided opportunities in my many and varied travels around the globe and triggered countless requests for me to write them down – possibly as a ruse to shut me up.

Being of literal mind (and shrinking pc storage space) I have finally done just that.

Some of these I feel do need the punch line spelled out and some don't, however, the vast majority of them remain what they are, corny jokes, handed down from generation to generation.

Huge thanks to everyone who has patiently (or impatiently) listened to any of these in the past and to Mark Gracey and the team at HotCake Marketing in Windsor for their cover artwork.

And so, taking absolutely no responsibility for the entertaining nature of this material (and without intentionally breaching any copyright to which these bon mots may be attributable), here is my treasured collection of clean, yet cringe-worthy jokes, puns, poems, batty books and other oddities which make up The Book of Cringe.

How does Moses make his tea?
Hebrews it.

How does the sea shore stay so clean?
Beachcombing.

What do you call a sad raspberry?
A blueberry.

How did Moses manage to read at night?
He had the Israelites.

A man with Dyslexia man walks into a bra.

When you've seen one shopping centre, you've seen a mall.

Chemistry teacher: "What is irony?"
Student: "Irony is when something has the chemical symbol Fe."

How many actors does it take to change a light bulb?
One. They don't like to share the spotlight.

What is the difference between The Rolling Stones and a Scottish shepherd?
One sings "Hey you get off my cloud" and the other sings "Hey, McLeod, get off my ewe."

"Doctor, Doctor, I keep singing Tom Jones songs."
"It's not unusual."

Confucius say wise man never play leapfrog with unicorn.

Knock! Knock!
Who's there?
Waiter.
Waiter who?
Water minute while I do up my shoelace.

A woman walks into a pub and asks the barman for a double entendre.
So he gave her one

A man walks into a pub with a roll of tarmac under his arm and says: "A pint please and one for the road."

A three-legged dog goes into a saloon in the Old West, drags himself up to the bar and says: "I'm looking for the man who shot my paw."

I wish I had been born 1000 years ago.
Why?
Just think of all the history that I wouldn't have to learn.

What do you call a baby whale?
A little squirt.

Did you hear about the man who was scared of a fat men in red, with long white beards?
He had Clause-trophobia.

I say, I say, I say.
My wife and I just went to Holland.
Utrecht?
No. We went by air.

Did you hear about the Dutch girl with inflatable shoes?
She's popped her clogs.

Roses are red,
Violets are blue,
They both smell quite nice,
Unlike you.

Why did Beethoven sell his chickens?
They kept saying Bach, Bach.

What do you get if you cross a stegosaurus with a firework?
Dino-mite.

How do you make a Swiss role?
Push him down a hill.

How to you make a French wine?
Steal his onions.

How do you make a venetian blind?
Poke him in the eyes.

What do you call a man in Prague who is thrown out of a night club?
A bounced Czech.

Knock! Knock!
Who's there?
Theodore.
Theodore who?
Theodore is stuck and I can't open it.

Which King invented the fireplace?
Alfred the Grate.

Why can't athletes listen to music?
Because they always want to break the record.

"Do you have a four volt, two watt lamp?"
"For what?"
"No... two."
"Two what?"
"Yes."
"No."

A backward poet writes inverse.

Why do lifeboats have soap and flannels in them?
To help shipwreck survivors wash themselves ashore

What do you call an elf with a skin disease?
A leper-chaun.

Why couldn't the life guard save the hippie?
He was too far out, man.

Waiter! Waiter!
Your tie is in my soup!
That's all right, sir, it's not silk.

How did Julius Caesar know the weather was bad outside?
Because one of his soldiers came into his tent and said "Hail, Caesar."

Six of the best from Star Trek

1. How many ears does Captain Kirk have?
    Three. A left ear, a right ear and a final front ear.

2. If Mr Spock has pointed ears, what kind of ears does Scotty have?
    Engineers.

3. Why couldn't the Vulcan see?
    He had dirty spocktacles.

4. What did Spock find in Kirk's lavatory?
    The captain's log.

5. Captain Kirk: "Very funny, Scotty. Now beam down my clothes."

6. What is the similarity between loo paper and the Starship Enterprise?
    They both travel round Uranus.

Knock! Knock!
Who's there?
Ulaanbaatar.
Ulaanbaatar who?
I knew that wasn't going to make a good punchline.

What do you call a broken can opener?
A can't opener.

What is red and doesn't exist?
No tomatoes.

How does an octopus go into battle?
Well-armed.

What type of music are balloons scared of?
Pop music.

Why should you learn sign language?
It's very handy.

Confucius say man who live in glass house should change in basement.

What underwear does a mermaid use?
An alge-bra.

What do you call an Elf walking backwards?
A fle.

What do dwarves and midgets have in common?
Little.

"Doctor, Doctor, I feel like a pair of curtains."
"Pull yourself together."

Did you hear about the librarian crushed by a load of books?
He only had his shelf to blame.

How does a lion like his meat?
Roar.

What did one chimney say to the other chimney?
You're too young to smoke.

BATTY BOOKS (1)

1960s fashion by Minnie Skirt
A day at the beach by C Side
Baby's revenge by Nora Titsov
Bad haircuts by Shaun Head
Bathroom disaster by Ivor Leak
Beginners' cookery lesson by Egon Chips
Bell ringing by Paul Rope
Blood suckers (part I) by Amos Quito
Blood suckers (part II) by Anne Othamosquito
Blood suckers (part III) by Andy Nuthamosquito
Blood suckers (part IV) by Stella Nuthamosquito
Blowing up buildings by D Molition
Boasting by Ivor Biggun
Brainless by M T Head
Breakfast recipes by Egon Toast
Breezes by Wynn D Weather
Brown specs on the wall by Hu Flung Dung
Cannibals by Henrietta Mann
Caring for parrots by L O Polly
Cliff Tragedy by Eileen Dover
Defrosting cattle by Thora Herd
Dentistry for beginners by Phil McAvity
Diets for dogs by Nora Bone
End of term by C Myra Port

How many road side workers does it take to change a lightbulb?
Five. One to do it and four to lean on their spades and watch

On how many chimneys does Father Christmas need to practise before Christmas Eve?
Stacks.

A circus performer named Brian
Smiled riding Ryan the lion
They came back from the ride
With young Brian inside
And a smile on the face of old Ryan.

Why didn't they play cards on the Ark?
Because Noah was standing on the deck.

What makes music on your head?
A head band.

What did the cobbler say to the stray dog?
"Shoe!"

What do you call a song sung in a Rolls Royce?
A cartoon.

Have you heard the one about the chiropodist?
It's a bit corny.

Did you hear about the wood carver?
He made his living whittle by whittle.

Confucius say man who jump off cliff leap to conclusion.

Who is the best babysitter mentioned in the Bible?
David, because he rocked Goliath to a very deep sleep.

Why is Miss Piggy's engagement so long?
Her fiancé is afraid of Kermitment.

What has forty feet and sings?
A choir.

What do you call a ferocious nude?
A grizzly bare.

Why are pirates such good singers?
They can hit the high Cs.

Did you hear about the musical about puns, with no orchestra score?
It was a play on words.

Did you hear about the out of work contortionist?
He was struggling to make ends meet.

Waiter! Waiter!
Do you call this a three-course meal?
That's right, sir. Two chips and a pea.

How many people can you get in a Honda?
Twelve – in the Bible the apostles were all in one Accord.

What do cats have for breakfast?
Mewsli.

Did you hear about the fire at the circus?
It was in tents.

Did you hear about the psychic dwarf who escaped
from prison?
The newspaper headlines said: 'small medium at large.'

Why were British Empire builders like ants?
They lived in colonies.

I say, I say, I say.
My wife caught a chill in the Gulf.
Qatar?
Yes, she was full of phlegm.

Did you hear about the actress who saw her first
strands of grey hair?
She thought she'd dye.

Knock! Knock!
Who's there?
Interrupting cow.
Interrupting c...
MOO!!!

Who was the best comedian in the Bible?
Samson - he brought the house down.

What do you call a murderer with fibre?
A cereal killer.

What is the difference between a fish and a piano?
You can't tuna fish.

What do clouds use for underwear?
Thunder pants.

Why did the loo roll go downstairs?
It was looking for the bottom.

One boy to another: "What would you do if a bird
plopped on your head?"
Second boy: "I wouldn't go out with her again."

What do you do when your lettuce has a fit?
Make a seizure salad.

Is there a motorbike in the Bible?
Yes. David's triumph was heard throughout the land.

What part of a chicken is musical?
The drumstick.

Why does moon rock taste better than earth rock?
It's meteor.

What does a clock do when it is hungry?
It goes back four seconds.

"Doctor, Doctor, I've lost my memory."
"When did this happen?"
"When did what happen?

What do you call the best butter on the farm?
A goat.

How does the man in the moon cut his hair?
Eclipse it.

Why don't they serve beer at maths club?
Because you can't drink and derive.

What is the most musical part of a fish?
The scales.

Did you hear about the Mexican train killer?
He had a loco motive.

What do you call a baby monkey?
A chimp off the old block.

Why did the singer take a ladder to choir practice?
To reach the high notes.

One.
How many mind readers does it take to change a
lightbulb?

E-flat walks into a pub and the barman says: "Sorry,
but we don't serve minors."

Why don't kleptomaniacs like puns?
They take things literally.

Knock! Knock!
Who's there?
I'm a pile up.
I'm a pile up who?
Oh dear!

What's yellow and dangerous?
Shark infested custard.

What was Bruce Lee's favourite drink?
Wataaah.

What do you call a mushroom who parties all night?
A fun guy.

Where did the music teacher leave his keys?
In the piano.

Did you hear about the dyslexic devil worshipper?
He sold his soul to Santa.

Did you know that Moses is the biggest sinner in the
Bible?
He broke all 10 commandments when he threw down
the stone tablets.

What has four legs and an arm?
A Rottweiler.

What kind of shoes to ninjas wear?
Sneakers.

What do you call a sheep with no head and no legs?
A cloud.

At what time of day was Adam created?
A little before Eve.

What do they call vicars in Germany?
German Shepherds.

"Doctor, Doctor. Your receptionist says she met me at
the vegetarian club."
"What's wrong with that?"
"I've never seen herbivore."

What did the Eskimo get after sitting on the cold ice?
Polaroids.

What kind of music did the Pilgrims like?
Plymouth Rock.

What is green and hairy and goes up and down?
A gooseberry in a lift.

Waiter! Waiter!
Do you have frogs' legs?
Yes sir.
Well hop over there and get me my food please.

What game can you play with a wombat?
Wom.

Why is the beach wet?
Because the sea weed.

Knock! Knock!
Who's there?
Tank.
Tank who?
You're welcome

What is the similarity between school children at
half-term and a Scotsman with a cold?
The both have a week off.

What did Tarzan say to Jane when he got home?
"It's a jungle out there."

What do you call a map guide to Alcatraz?
A con-tour map.

What party games do cannibals play?
Swallow my leader.

Did you hear about the magician walking down the
street?
He turned into a shop.

How do you make a band stand?
Take away the chairs.

A boiled egg is hard to beat.

When does medicine get mentioned in the Bible?
When God gave Moses two tablets.

What kind of man was Ruth's husband before he got married?
Ruthless.

Did you hear about the constipated mathematician?
He worked it out with a pencil.

What is the definition of a polygon?
A dead parrot.

What did the Eskimo say when his kayak sank after he lit a fire in it to warm up?
"You can't have your kayak and heat it."

"Doctor, Doctor, I keep having déjà-vu."
"You said that to me yesterday."

Why did the lazy man want a job in the bakery?
So he could loaf around.

Did you hear about the Buddhist who refused his dentist's pain killer during a root canal?
He wanted to transcend dental medication.

Two Aerials met on a roof, fell in love and were married.
The ceremony was rubbish but the reception was excellent.

What do you call an expensive dog?
A dear hound.

What is the last thing to go through a bug's mind as it
hits a windscreen?
His bum.

A man walks into see the psychiatrist wearing only a
pair of shorts made from cling film.
The psychiatrist says: "Well, I can clearly see you're
nuts."

Two elephants walk off a cliff.
Boom! Boom!

What's the best way to study the Bible?
Luke into it.

Waiter! Waiter!
Do you have frogs' legs?
No Madam. This is how I walk.

What is brown and sounds like a bell?
Dung.

What do you call a dinosaur who disturbs you in your
bed?
A dinosnorus.

A neutron walks into a pub and asks for a beer.
"How much is that please?" it asks.
"For you?" replies the barman. "No charge."

Knock! Knock!
Who's there?
Syria.
Syria who?
Seriously! Don't you know me?

Two large men were drinking in a pub and one says to the other: "Your round."
"But you are obese," replies the other.

What do you call a soaking wet bear?
A drizzly.

Who introduced the first walking stick in the Bible?
Eve when she presented Adam a little Cain.

Two silk worms had a race.
And ended up in a tie.

What happened to the plant in the maths teacher's garden?
It grew square roots.

Two sharks were eating a clown fish, when one turns to the other and says: "Does this taste funny?"

Why was the kangaroo the most miserable animal on the ark?
Her children had to play inside in the rain.

Why were the horses so negative?
They are always saying "neigh."

"Doctor, Doctor, I feel like a pack of cards."
"I'll deal with you later."

What did the artist say on finishing his Bas carving?
What a relief.

Did you hear about the patient whose doctor told him
to rub goose fat into his back?
He went downhill fast.

What do you call a woman with tiles on her head?
Ruth.

Why were Andrew, James, John and Peter the best
letter writers in the Bible?
Because as fishermen they learned how to drop a line.

Police arrested two teenagers for drinking battery acid
and eating fireworks.
They charged one and let the other one off.

A man walks into a pub and had the ploughman's
lunch.
The ploughman wasn't happy.

Man to other man whose dog won't stop barking:
"Can't you shut him up?"
"Sorry," replies the dog's owner. "He's a cross breed."

What do you call a man with a legal document on his
head?
Will.

Did you hear about the man who went shopping for
some camouflage trousers?
He couldn't find any.

What US state is mentioned in the Bible?
Arkansas - Noah looked out from the ark and saw.

What is the definition of acoustic?
A Scottish dairy farmer's crook.

Four fonts walk into a pub and the barman says:
"Get out! We don't want your type in here."

I say, I say, I say.
My husband's just bought a new hat.
Fedora?
No, it's for himself.

Did you hear about the stupid hunt saboteur?
He went out the night before and shot the fox.

How many monkeys does it take to change a lightbulb?
Two. One to change it the other to scratch his bum.

Did you hear about the gangster who pulls up the back
of people's underpants?
He's called Wedgie Kray.

Police have arrested the Duracell Bunny.
He's been charged with battery.

"Doctor, Doctor, I keep dropping things."
"Don't worry, it's not catching."

What do you call a man with a kilt on his head?
Scott.

Why should you always swim backstroke after lunch?
You shouldn't swim on a full stomach.

Knock! Knock!
Who's there?
I eat mop.
I eat mop who?
How revolting.

Did you hear about the chess grandmasters at a table
with a checked tablecloth?
It took one of them two hours to pass the salt.

What did the greengrocer say when he ran out of
onions?
"That's shallot."

Confucius say man who go to bed with itchy bum wake
up with sticky fingers.

How did Mary show that Jesus was a gift to the world?
She wrapped him.

Waiter! Waiter!
Your thumb's in my soup!
Thank you for your concern, but it's not hot.

Did you hear about the man who painted his wife in oils?
She looked like a sardine.

What has four wheels and flies?
A dustbin lorry.

To err is human, to moo bovine.

What note do you get if you drop a piano down a mineshaft?
A-flat miner.

What do you call a woman with a tortoise on her head?
Shelley.

Did you hear about the ice-cream seller found dead in his van all covered in hundreds and thousands?
Police think he topped himself.

If April showers bring May flowers, what do May flowers bring?
Pilgrims.

Why was the River of Jordan angry?
Because someone crossed it.

Why were snakes the smartest animals?
You can't pull their legs.

There was a young girl in the choir
Whose voice rose higher and higher
'Til it reached such a height
That it was out of sight
And they found it stuck on the spire.

"Doctor, Doctor, can you clear my spots?"
"I don't make rash promises."

What do you call a man with a rabbit up his bottom?
Warren.

Did you hear about the man found buried under a huge
pile of cornflakes
Police are looking for a cereal killer.

What do we have that Adam never had?
Ancestors.

Why was Joseph the straightest man in the Bible?
Because Pharaoh made a ruler of him.

How do you make seven into an even number?
Take the S out.

Knock! Knock!
Who's there?
Isabelle.
Isabelle who?
Isabelle necessary on a bicycle?

How do hedgehogs make love?
Very carefully.

Why did the man sleep under his car?
He had to wake up oily in the morning.

Why did the one armed man cross the road?
To get to the second hand shop.

What do you call a nun with a washing machine on her head?
Sister Matic.

Where do you find a donkey with no legs?
Where you left it.

How many censors does it take to change a lightbulb?
One. They --- -------- -- ------.

Roses are red,
Violets are blue,
I was born beautiful,
What happened to you?

Why was Solomon the wisest man in the world?
Because he had so many wives to advise him.

What do you call a Russian with a cold?
Ivan Astikov.

Why is a passionate kiss like a spider's web?
It leads to the undoing of a fly.

What is black and shoots out of the ground saying "knickers!"?
Crude oil.

What do you call a dinosaur that smashes everything in its path?
Tyrannosaurus wrecks.

What kind of lights did Noah have on the ark?
Flood lights.

Did you hear about the man who went to a fancy dress party in gooseberries and cream?
He looked like a fool.

Waiter! Waiter!
Do you have soup on the menu?
No sir, I have wiped it off.

A man was invited to a fancy dress party as an Italian island.
His friends said: "Don't be Sicily."

Why was Job the most successful physician in the Bible?
He had the most patience.

A male streaker ran past two old ladies on a park bench.
One had a stroke, but the other couldn't reach.

How do you squash a ghost?
With a spirit level.

Knock! Knock!
Who's there?
Spell.
Spell who?
W. H. O.

Why did the unemployed man get excited while looking through his Bible?
He thought he saw a Job.

What happened when Bramley married the Pink Lady?
They lived appley ever after.

What do you call a man with no legs, water-skiing?
Skip.

How does the ocean say hello?
It waves.

"Doctor, Doctor, I think I'm a dog."
"Hop on couch and I'll have a look at you."
"I'm not allowed on the couch."

Those who get too big for their britches will be exposed in the end.

Did you know that diarrhoea is genetic?
It runs in your jeans.

Which farm animals are famous artists?
Vincent van Goat and Pablo Pigaso.

Don't ever mention the number 288.
It is two gross.

What did the scarecrow get a pay rise?
He was outstanding in his field.

Did you hear the joke about the pizza?
Actually it's a bit too cheesey.

What if there were no hypothetical situations?

Why are politicians and nappies alike?
They both need regular changing and for the same
reason.

René Descartes walks into a pub and the barman asks
if he wants anything.
"I think not," replies Descartes, then disappears.

What do you call a fairy that doesn't wash?
Stinker Bell.

Waiter! Waiter!
Will my pizza be long?
No sir, it will be round.

Where ban you buy four suits for a pound?
A pack of cards.

What do you do when your chair breaks?
Call the chairman.

What happened when a ship carrying red paint collided with a ship carrying blue paint?
Their crews were marooned.

Did you hear about the man who was addicted to washing with soap?
He's clean now.

What do you call a man with a load of hay on his head?
Rick.

Knock! Knock!
Who's there?
Ivan
Ivan who?
Ivan awful headache after reading these jokes.

What foot complaint did Sampson have?
Falling arches.

"Doctor, Doctor, I think I am a caterpillar."
"You will soon change."

How do dinosaurs pay their bills?
With Tyrannosaurus cheques.

Which animal didn't Noah trust?
The cheetah.

Who was the most famous runner in the Bible?
Adam was, because he was first in the human race.

What do you call a dinosaur that wears a cowboy hat and boots?
Tyrannosaurus Tex.

What animal has the smallest appetite?
A moth - he just eats holes.

Teacher: "Why are you doing your multiplication on the floor?"
Student: "You told me not to use tables."

How do we know Cain took a nap when he left Eden?
He went to the land of Nod.

What do you get if you cross a chicken with a cement mixer?
A brick layer.

What do you call a dinosaur that never takes a bath?
Stinkosaurus.

What do you get if you cross an elephant and a kangaroo?
Gigantic holes over Australia.

Who invented fractions?
Henry the eighth.

What insect went to Egypt on a donkey?
A flea - the angel told Joseph to take Mary, the baby and flea into Egypt.

The short fortune teller who escaped from prison was a small medium at large.

What do you get when you cross a stream and a brook?
Wet feet.

What did one ghost say to the other ghost?
Do you believe in people?

Knock! Knock!
Who's there?
Snow.
Snow who?
Snow business like show business.

Do you serve crabs?
Yes sir, we serve anyone.

Knock! Knock!
Who's there?
Snow.
Snow who?
Snow use, I've forgotten the rest of this joke.

What do you call a man with a casserole dish on his head?
Stu.

"Doctor, Doctor, I think I am slowing up the traffic?
"It'll pass."

What bird placed Jonah in the belly of the fish?
A swallow.

Psychiatrist to cured patient: "Why are you so sad?"
Patient: "Yesterday I was God. Today I am nobody."

How do you ask a dinosaur out?
Tea, Rex?

What kind of cats like to go bowling?
Alley cats.

Confucius say man who drop watch in toilet have crap time.

What has six eyes but can't see?
Three blind mice.

I say, I say, I say.
My wife's family build environmental vehicles off the coast of Africa.
Madagascar?
No they're all electric.

What do you call a ghost's mother and father?
Transparents.

How many surrealist painters does it take to change a lightbulb?
Fish.

What do you get when you cross poison ivy with a four-leaf clover?
A rash of good luck.

How do we know the Indians were the first people in North America?
They had reservations.

What do you call an elephant in a phone box?
Stuck.

What is the best thing to do if you find a gorilla in your bed?
Sleep somewhere else.

Doctor: "I have got some good news and some bad news for you."
Patient: "Give me the bad news, first."
Doctor: "I am afraid we cut off the wrong leg."
Patient: "What's the good news?"
Doctor: "Your other one is getting much better."

Why is a maths book always unhappy?
Because it always has lots of problems.

What is grey, eats fish, and lives in Washington, D.C.?
The Presidential Seal.

What do you call a man with a double decker bus on his head?
The deceased.

Did you hear about the dyslexic, agnostic insomniac?
He lay awake all night worrying about the existence of dog.

What is green and loud?
A frog horn.

How do they elect the leader of the Catholic faith?
When one dies another Pope's along.

Did you hear about the animal park that only had one small dog in it?
It was a shih tzu.

"Doctor, Doctor, my husband is so ill, is there any hope?"
"That depends on what you are hoping for."

What is a superhero's favourite drink?
Fruit punch.

Did you hear about the dog who gave birth to puppies near the road?
Police charged her with littering.

How long did Cain hate his brother?
As long as he was Abel.

How many archaeologists does it take to change a lightbulb?
Three. One to change it and two to discuss the age of the old one.

What is round and is always bad tempered?
A vicious circle.

Where do fortune tellers dance?
At the crystal ball.

Waiter! Waiter!
What is this in my soup?
I'm not sure, sir, I can't tell one bug from another.

What do you call Father Christmas' helpers?
Subordinate clauses.

How do you make an egg laugh?
Tell it a yolk.

What did one maths book say to the other?
Don't bother me now, I've got my own problems.

Knock! Knock!
Who's there?
Ivor.
Ivor who?
Ivor you let me in or I'll climb through your window.

How does a pig go to hospital?
By hambulance.

Which bird can lift the most?
A crane.

How do they make Holy Water?
Get regular water and boil the devil out of it.

What bone will a dog never eat?
A trombone.

What did the tie say to the hat?
You go on ahead and I'll hang around for a while.

What do you call a Welshman, covered in treacle with a stick up his bum?
Taffy apple.

What does a house wear?
Address.

What was King Arthur's favourite game?
Knights and crosses.

"Doctor, Doctor, I've swallowed my pocket money."
"Drink this and let's see if there's any change in the morning."

What do you call a man between two houses?
Ali.

What can you hold but not touch?
A conversation.

What did one magnet say to the other?
I find you very attractive.

What did the rug say to the floor?
I've got you covered.

What do boxers drink?
Punch.

How do you cut a wave?
With a sea saw.

What do skunks do when they get angry?
They raise a stink

What's the longest word in the dictionary?
Rubber-band - because it stretches.

Knock! Knock!
Who's there?
Ketchup.
Ketchup who?
Ketchup with me and I'll let you know.

When does a dialect become a language?
When its speakers get an army and a navy.

What do you call a small fish magician?
A magic carpet.

What kind of underwear do journalists wear?
News briefs.

When was cooked meat first mentioned in the Bible?
When Noah took Ham into the ark.

What did Tennessee?
The same as Arkansas.

Where do maths teachers go on vacation?
Times Square.

How to you make a fire with two sticks?
Make sure one of them is a match.

What do you call a place where everyone drives a pink car?
A pink carnation.

What do you call a place where everyone drives a red car?
A red carnation.

What do you call a place where everyone lives in their cars?
An incarnation.

Did you hear about the professor who discovered that his theory of earthquakes was on shaky ground?

What did Adam say to his wife on 24 December?
"It's Christmas, Eve."

"Doctor, Doctor, I feel like a wigwam in the morning and a big top in the afternoon."
"Relax, you are too tense."

What do you get if you cross a boxer with an artist?
Mohamed Dali.

Where are you most likely to get a puncture?
At a fork in the road.

Why is an Eskimo's bed cold?
Because they have blankets of snow.

How do you organise a party for an astronomer?
Planet early.

Waiter! Waiter!
Have you got asparagus?
We don't serve sparrows and my name isn't Gus.

Why was Pharaoh's daughter the greatest female
businessperson in the Bible?
She went down to the bank of the Nile and drew out a
little prophet.

Knock! Knock!
Who's there?
Soup.
Soup who?
Superman.

What kind of music do you hear in space?
Neptunes.

How does a train eat?
It chew chews.

What do you call a man with a wig on his head?
Aaron.

Where was King Solomon's temple?
By the side of his head.

I say, I say, I say.
My wife's parents are from Croatia.
Split?
No, they're still together.

What did the artist say to the dentist?
Matisse hurt.

"A man just came into the gallery asking if your
paintings would increase in value after your death.
Unfortunately he was your doctor."

Optician: "Have your eyes been checked before?"
Patient: "No. They've always been one colour."

What do you call a snowman in July?
A puddle.

Oxygen and magnesium have got together.
OMg!

What is the difference between a mathematician and a
philosopher?
The mathematician only needs paper, pencil, and a
trash bin for his work - the philosopher can do without
the trash bin.

Why did the artist think he might go to prison?
Because he had been framed.

What is red and smells like blue paint?
Red paint.

Which letters do Tuesday, Thursday, Friday and
Saturday have in common?
None – they don't have c, o, m, or n in them.

What do you call dangerous precipitation?
A rain of terror.

Little birdie flying high,
Dropped a message from the sky,
Now I am big and didn't cry,
But I did thank God that cows don't fly.

Why can't you hear a pterodactyl on the loo?
Because the P is silent.

Why didn't the shrimp share?
He was a little shellfish.

"Doctor, Doctor, I've jelly and custard in one ear and
sponge in the other."
"You are a trifle deaf."

Why did Adam tell his children they lived in poverty?
"Your mother ate us out of house and home.

How much to pirates pay for corn?
A buccaneer.

Why does a milking stool have three legs?
Because the cow has the udder.

Why do cows wear bells?
Because their horns don't work.

A Freudian slip is when you say one thing but mean your mother.

Waiter! Waiter!
What is this cockroach doing in my ice cream?
Skiing?

How do we know Peter the Apostle was a good fisherman?
By his net income.

What do you call a woman with a screwdriver in one hand, a knife in the other, a pair of scissors between the toes on her left foot, and a corkscrew between the toes on her right foot?
A Swiss Army wife.

Knock! Knock!
Who's there?
Smell mop.
Smell mop who?
No thanks.

What was Camelot?
A place where you parked your camel.

What do you get if you sit under a cow?
A pat on the head.

Did you hear about the man whose beret blew off in a
cow pasture?
He tried on five before he found his own.

Is tennis mentioned in the bible?
Yes, when Joseph served in Pharaoh's court.

What do you call a nun who sleepwalks?
A roaming catholic.

How many crime writers does it take to change a
lightbulb?
Two. One to change the bulb and the other to give it a
clever little twist at the end.

If the answer is 'Rudolph Hesse', vat is the qvestion?
Vich reindeer hesse a red nose?

A horse walked into a pub and the barman says:
"Why the long face?"

Why did the chicken cross the road?
To get to the other side.

What was Noah's real job?
Arkitect.

Why did the cow cross the road?
To get to the udder side.

Did you hear about the crash between two vans
carrying tortoises and terrapins?
It was a turtle disaster.

"Doctor, Doctor, I've got acute appendicitis."
"And I've got a lovely dimple."

How did the hairdresser revive the dead rabbit?
With some hare restorer.

What do you call a fly with no wings?
A walk.

What did zero say eight?
Nice belt.

Why did Eve want to move to New York?
She fell for the Big Apple.

Knock! Knock!
Who's there?
Lettuce.
Lettuce who?
Lettuce in it is freezing out here.

What five-letter word becomes shorter when you add two letters to it?
Short.

What did one goldfish say to the other goldfish when they were in a tank?
"Do you know how to drive this?"

Teacher: "Who write the famous book about the French invasion of Russia?"
Pupil: "Warren Peace?"

"Fetch me a crocodile sandwich!"
"And make it snappy!"

What is the difference between Batman and a thief?
Batman can go into a store without robin.

A good pun is its own reword.

Did you know that Noah was the first merchant banker?
He floated his stock when everyone else was in liquidation

What do you call a female elf?
A shelf.

"It's raining cats and dogs outside."
"I know, I just stepped in poodle."

Where do frogs get an eye test?
The hopticians.

Do you need a boat to save two of every animal?
I Noah guy.

What is the fastest tea cake in the world?
Scone.

"Doctor, Doctor, the medicine you gave me isn't working.
Is there anything else I can try?"
"You could try filling out this tax return form."
"Why will that help me, Doctor?"
"Some of my patients say it gives them relief."

How many magicians does it take to change a
lightbulb?
It depends upon what you want to change it into.

How do you titillate an ocelot?
Oscillate its tit a lot.

What do you call a boomerang which doesn't come back?
A stick.

Did Adam have a date with Eve?
No – an apple.

Waiter! Waiter!
I wish to complain to the chef about this disgusting
meal.
I'm afraid you'll have to wait, sir, he's just popped out for
dinner.

How do you catch a squirrel?
Climb up a tree and act like a nut.

Which cake wanted to rule the world?
Attilla the bun.

Knock! Knock!
Who's there?
Sarah.
Sarah who?
Sarah doctor in the house, please, I'm not feeling well?

What has one horn and gives milk?
A milk float.

Why didn't Noah go fishing?
He only had two worms.

What do you call an underweight religious guru with
calloused feet and bad breath?
A super calloused fragile mystic hexed by halitosis.

How do you make a cat go woof?
Soak in petrol.

What is grey and has a trunk?
A mouse going on holiday.

What is brown and has a trunk?
A mouse coming back from holiday.

When does a horse talk?
Whinny wants to.

I say, I say, I say.
My wife's just admitted smoking a joint near
Manchester.
In Hale?
She says not.

The amazing Wizard of Oz
Retired from business because
With advances in science
To most of his clients
He wasn't the wiz that he was.

What kind of horse only goes out after dark?
A night mare.

Why was Jonah scared of the sea?
There was something fishy about

Confucius say man who drive like hell bound to get
there.

What do you call a dinosaur with an extensive
vocabulary?
A thesaurus.

Roses are red,
Violets are blue,
Some poems rhyme,
But this one doesn't.

Why do ducks have webbed feet?
For stamping out forest fires.

Why do giraffes have such long necks?
Because they have very smelly feet.

Why do elephants have flat feet?
For stamping out burning ducks.

"Doctor, Doctor, I can't drink my medicine after my
bath as you instructed."
"I didn't mean drink the bath first!"

What kind of fly has a frog in its throat?
A hoarse fly.

Knock! Knock!
Who's there?
Little old lady.
Little old lady who?
I didn't know you could yodel.

Why do elephants all have grey trunks?
They belong to the same swimming club.

What do you get if you cross a math teacher with a
crab?
Snappy answers.

Did you hear about the frog's car when it broke down?
It was toad away.

Did you hear about the snail who lost his shell?
He became sluggish.

Who is the strongest animal?
A snail because it carries its home.

What do frogs order when they go to a restaurant?
French Flies.

What do you call a gun with three barrels?
A trifle.

What goes 99 thump, 99 thump, 99 thump?
A centipede with a wooden leg.

What do penguins wear on their heads?
Ice caps.

When did the fly fly?
When the spider spied her.

What do you call a nervous witch?
A twitch.

What's worse than finding a maggot in your apple?
Finding half a maggot.

What did the dog say to the flea?
Stop bugging me.

Who was George Washington's army entertainer?
Laughayette.

What did the duck say when she bought some new lipstick?
"Put it on my bill."

Waiter! Waiter!
What is this fly doing in my soup?
It looks like the back-stroke.

How do painters say goodbye in Japan?
Cyan-ara.

Knock! Knock!
Who's there?
Russia
Russia who?
Russia round the back and see who's there.

What was Bruce Wayne's favourite part in cricket?
Batting.

A horse goes into a pub and orders a whisky. "We've got a whisky named after you," says the barman. "What?" asks the horse. "Eric?"

What do you call a German hairdresser?
Herr Kutz.

Why did Renoir become an Impressionist?
For the Monet.

Teacher: "Is there an English word that uses all the vowels and y?
Student: "Unquestionably."

A camel goes into a pub and the barman says: "We've got cigarettes named after you."
"What?" asks the camel. "Camilla?"

A panda goes into a pub and says: "Please may I have .... a .... pint?"
"Certainly," says the barman, "but why the big pause?"
"I'm a panda."

The maths teacher went crazy with the blackboard and did a number on it.

What did the skunk say when it walked into a pub?
"Where did everybody go?"

Waiter! Water!
My meal is off.
Where to?

Confucius say person who listen to railway line for train get splitting headache.

What do you call a woman with one leg shorter than the other?
Eileen.

What do you call a Chinese woman with one leg shorter than the other?
Irene.

What would the Earth be without Art?
Eh.

What did the termite say when it walked into a pub?
"Is the bartender here?"

What begins with T, ends with T and has T in it?
A teapot.

An Englishman, Irishman and a Scotsman walked into
a pub and the barman says "Is this some kind of a
joke?"

Knock! Knock!
Who's there?
Radio.
Radio who?
Radio not here I come.

What do you call a woman with a twig on her head?
Hazel.

What don't you say when you comfort a grammar
teacher?
"There, their, they're."

How do you spell mousetrap?
C A T.

"You have 24 hours to live."
"Can I have a second opinion?"
"You are also ugly."

A sandwich walks into a pub and the barman says:
"Sorry, but we don't serve food here."

A screwdriver walks into a pub and the barman says:
"We have a drink named after you."
"What?" asks the screwdriver. "David?"

A snowball walks into a pub and the barman says: "We
have a drink named after you."
"What?" asks the snowball. "Gareth?"

A man walks into a pub and asks for some helicopter
flavoured crisps.
"Sorry, we don't have those here," says the barman.
"OK," replies the man, "I'll have some plain ones,
please."

How many therapists does it take to change a
lightbulb?
One. But the lightbulb has to want to change.

What is the only English word pronounced the same
when you remove its last four letters?
Queue.

How does King Wenceslas like his pizza?
Deep pan crisp and even.

What kind of hair do oceans have?
Wavy.

Have you heard about the idiot who always says "no"?
No.

What did the painter do before going to bed?
Drew the curtains.

A LIST OF NATIONS (1)

Abomination	- a place for the disliked
Alienation	- ET's home
Assignation	- where people only meet in secret
Carbonation	- where the effervescent live
Combination	- where people like to get together
Consternation	- for the bewildered
Cross-pollination	- where angry parrots live
Culmination	- for people at their peak
Declination	- for people on a downward slope
Denomination	- inhabited by the pious
Designation	- inhabited by those who need classification
Destination	- where no one lives but lots of people visit
Determination	- inhabited by the resolute
Discrimination	- where people are unfair
Dissemination	- a very scattered population
Divination	- inhabited by fortune-tellers
Domination	- where people are under the thumb of a tyrant
Donation	- a place for the giving
Elimination	- for those who have dropped out
Examination	- dreaded by students
Explanation	- a home for teachers
Extermination	- where people are tough on rats
Fascination	- where there are the greatest number of marriages
Germination	- where people grow

Knock! Knock!
Who's there?
Who.
Who who?
Is there an owl in here?

What do history teachers make when they want to get
together?
Dates.

"Doctor, Doctor, I am addicted to brake fluid."
"You can stop any time."

Thomas Edison walks into a pub and orders a pint.
The bartender says, "I'll serve you a beer, just don't get
any ideas."

What is the definition of grammar?
The difference between knowing your rubbish from
you're rubbish.

A man walks into a pub with a baby seal under his arm
and says: "A gin and tonic for me and a Canadian club
on the rocks for him."

A gossip is someone with a great sense of rumour.

Knock! Knock!
Who's there?
Luke.
Luke who?
Look through the window and see for yourself.

A man with dyslexia walks into a bra.

Last December I painted a girl in the nude.
I almost froze to death.

Waiter! Waiter!
What is this?
It's bean salad, sir.
Yes, but what is it now?

What do you call a woman with no arms or legs in river?
Flo.

A man with amnesia walks into a pub and the barman
says: "What's your poison?"
"I am not sure," replies the man. "I have trouble
remembering things."
"Oh really?" asks the barman. "Like what?"

What English word begins and ends with the same
three letters in the same order?
Underground.

Why is it easy to get into Florida?
Because there are so many keys.

A man walks into a pub with a wombat under his arm
and the barman says: "Where did you get that
monkey?"
"It's not a monkey," replies the man. "It is a wombat."
"Excuse me," says the barman, "I was talking to the
wombat."

A jump lead goes into a pub and the barman says:
"I'll serve you, but don't start anything."

What do you call a man with a stamp on his head?
Frank.

Name a bus you can't ride on?
A syllabus.

What letter of the alphabet has got lots of water?
The C.

What letter of the alphabet is always waiting in order?
The Q.

Knock! Knock!
Who's there?
Medina
Medina who?
Medina's on the table so I've got to go.

A man walks into a pub with a piece of tarmac under
his arm and says: "A pint of beer please and one for the
road."

Some black tarmac and some red tarmac were drinking
in a pub when in came some green tarmac.
"Watch out for him," says the red tarmac, "he's a cycle
path."

A hangover is the wrath of grapes.

Patient: "Doctor, Doctor. I have a banana stuck up my nose, a turnip in my ear and mashed potato in my eye."
Doctor: "Well, first of all, you are going to have to learn to eat more sensibly."

"Doctor, Doctor, people keep ignoring me."
"Next!"

Conversation between Vincent van Gogh and his friend in a pub.
"Fancy a pint, Vince?"
"No thanks, I've got one ear!"

I say, I say, I say.
My wife's just had an upset tummy on a trip to Laos.
Inkhazi?
For most of the holiday.

What is black and white and read all over?
A newspaper.

What do you call a woman with two pints of beer on her head?
Beatrix.

What do you call a woman with two pints of beer on her head, making something out of clay?
Beatrix Potter.

A drunk walks into a bar.
"Ouch!"

A skeleton walks into a pub and says barman:
"Please may I have a pint and a mop."

Why don't melons marry in Gretna Green?
They cantaloupe.

Confucius say man who cut self while shaving lose face.

Why shouldn't you wear Russian boxer shorts?
Chernobyl fallout.

Knock! Knock!
Who's there?
Mikey.
Mikey who.
Mikey doesn't fit in the lock.

Why aren't there any headache pills in the jungle?
Because the parrots-eat-'em-all.

How do you make toast in the jungle?
Pop two bits of bread under the gorilla.

What do you get if you add two apples and three apples?
A maths question.

Waiter! Waiter!
My plate is wet!
That is actually the soup.

What do you call a fish with no eye?
Fsh.

Where do you learn to make ice cream?
Sundae school.

What pudding roams wild in the Arctic?
Moose.

Why did the jelly baby go to school?
To try and become a Smartie.

Did you hear about the man who had two lenses on his head?
He made a spectacle of himself.

Doctor: "I have got some good news and some bad news."
Patient: "Give me the bad news first."
Doctor: "You are at death's door."
Patient: "What's the good news?"
Doctor: "I can pull you through."

What goes up and down but doesn't move?
Stairs.

Where should a 30 stone alien go?
On a diet.

What do you call a Grizzlie with no teeth?
A gummy bear.

What did one lavatory say to the other?
You look a bit flushed.

How many gardeners does it take to change a
lightbulb?
One. But he has to consider which bulb to use
depending upon the time of year.

Did you hear about the dull and dreary seaside town?
The tide went out and never came back.

A policeman said to a drunk in prison: "You've been
brought in for drinking."
"Great," replied the prisoner. "Mine's a pint."

What kind of cheese isn't yours?
Nacho cheese.

Why did the picture go to jail?
Because it was framed.

What has a tongue but cannot speak?
A shoe.

Where was the Magna Carta signed?
At the bottom.

She was an unrepentant whisky-maker but he loved her
still.

What is the definition of wasted energy?
Telling a hair-raising story to a bald man.

Why was the spaghetti locked out of his house?
He had gnocchi.

Why is marriage like game of poker?
You start with a pair and end with a full house.

What do you call a laughing knee?
Funny.

Knock! Knock!
Who's there?
Orange.
Orange who?
Orange you going to let me in?

What did one wall say to the other wall?
I'll meet you at the corner.

"Doctor, Doctor, I keep thinking I am a cowboy."
"How long have you felt like this?"
"About a yeehaa."

What did the paper say to the pencil?
Write on.

What on one elf say to the other elf?
"Small world, isn't it?"

How do you describe an elf who is a millionaire?
Welfy.

What do history teachers talk about on dates?
The good old days.

Waiter! Waiter!
There's a bird in my soup.
That's right, sir, it is bird's nest soup.

How many elves does it take to change a light bulb?
Ten. One to change it and nine to stand on each other's
shoulders so he can reach.

If athletes get athlete's foot, what do elves get?
Mistletoe.

Eleven elves were joined by one more.
He was the twelf.

On which side of Jack's house did the beanstalk grow?
The outside.

What kind of pet did Aladdin have?
A flying carpet.

Who wears a red cape and shouts "knickers" at the big
bad wolf?
Little Rude Riding Hood.

If Mississippi and Missouri both wore a New Jersey,
what did Delaware?
Idaho, Alaska.

Why did Robin Hood steal from the rich?
Because the poor didn't have any money.

Did you hear about the plastic surgeon?
He melted in front of a fire.

"Doctor, Doctor, I am a kleptomaniac."
"Have you taken anything for it?"
"A wallet, a briefcase and a pen."

What do you call a woman with a breeze on her head?
Gail.

Why did the two fours miss lunch?
They already ate.

How did the man get his name in lights all over the world?
He changed his name to Emergency Exit.

How do you start a bear race?
Ready! Teddy! Go!

What is a superhero's favourite part of a joke?
The punch line.

Knock! Knock!
Who's there?
Oman
Oman who?
Oman, these Knock! Knock! jokes are really bad!

What did the police do when the hares escaped from
the zoo?
They combed the area.

What do you call cows that are lying down?
Ground beef.

What do you get if you cross a cowboy with an
octopus?
Billy the squid.

What do you get if you cross a hen with a bedside clock?
An alarm cluck.

What do you get if you cross a kangaroo with an
octopus, a sheep and a zebra?
A striped, woolly jumper with eight sleeves

What should you do if a rhino charges you?
Pay it.

A man's home is his castle, in a manor of speaking.

Where are the Andes?
On the end of the armies.

What did one angel say to the other angel?
Halo.

Waiter! Waiter!
This soup tastes funny.
But you're not laughing?

What do you call a man who isn't religious?
Godfrey.

What do you call a man who comes through a student letterbox?
Grant.

What do you get if you cross a river with a bike?
Wet.

Who is the warmest athlete?
The long jumper.

What is wrapped in tin foil and lives in a bell tower?
The lunch pack of Notre Dame.

What gets wetter the more it dries?
A towel.

Why couldn't the sesame bun leave the casino?
He was on a roll.

"Doctor, Doctor, I feel like a bell."
"If you still feel like this tomorrow, give me a ring."

What did Cinderella say when her photos did not arrive?
"Someday my prints will come."

What do you call a man with no hair and a biscuit on his head?
Garibaldi.

Who was the biggest thief in history?
Atlas. He held up the whole world.

Knock! Knock!
Who's there?
Norma Lee.
Norma Lee who?
Norma Lee I don't knock on doors.

Why don't eggs like jokes?
They crack up at the punchlines.

Reading while sunbathing makes you well-red.

Why was the broom late?
Because it over swept.

Why is a small hotel like a pair of tight trousers?
No ballroom.

How many Blue Peter presenters does it take to screw
in a lightbulb?
Two. One to do it and the other to show you one they
made earlier.

Did you hear about the angry magician?
He pulled his hare out.

When called an idiot it is sometimes better to remain
silent, rather than open your mouth and remove all
doubt.

Why did the florist give up her job?
She saw there was no fuchsia in it.

Did you hear about the dentist who married the
manicurist?
They fought tooth and nail.

Why is a chicken crossing the road a beauty to behold?
It is poultry in motion.

I say, I say, I say.
My wife's just been on a sailing course in Poole.
In Dorset?
I think she would recommend it, yes.

What do you call a chicken in a shell suit?
An egg.

Why did the bank manager change jobs?
He lost interest.

Did you hear about the man who fell into an upholstery
machine?
He is fully recovered now.

Confucius say person who run behind car get
exhausted.

Did you hear about the man who fell onto a chainsaw
and lost the left side of his body?
He's all right now.

Waiter! Waiter!
There's a dead fly in my soup.
For that price you didn't expect a live one, did you?

What type of blood to pessimists have?
B-negative.

"Doctor, Doctor, I feel like a sheep."
"That is baaaad."

Did you hear about the thief who stole a calendar?
He got twelve months.

What city always cheats at exams?
Peking.

Did you hear about the theft of all the police loos?
They have nothing to go on.

What do you call a bear with no socks on?
Bare-foot.

Did you hear about the man who worked in a can
crushing factory?
He found his work depressing.

Why did the man lose his job at the blanket factory?
It folded.

What do elves sing to Father Christmas?
Freeze a jolly good fellow.

Knock! Knock!
Who's there?
Omelette.
Omelette who?
Omelette smarter than I look!

Why did the baker rob a bank?
He kneaded the dough.

Where do monsters live?
Monster-ocities.

What do you call a cow that can't make milk?
An udder failure.

Why did the baker have brown hands?
He needed a poo.

What do they do with dead chemists?
Barium.

Waiter! Waiter!
This coffee tastes like soap.
Then that must be tea, sir. The coffee tastes like glue.

Did you hear about the hole in the nudist camp wall?
Police are looking into it.

What do you call a Scottish cloakroom attendant?
Angus McCoatup.

To bed with the lark and up with the cock.

Did you hear about the thief who fell into wet cement?
He became a hardened criminal.

Roses are red,
Violets are blue,
What I thought was Vaseline,
Turned out to be glue.

Why do we never have a shortage of maths teachers?
Because they always multiply.

Did you hear about the man who jumped off a bridge
in Paris?
He was in Seine.

Practice safe eating - always use condiments.

Why was King Arthur's army too tired to fight?
They had too many sleepless knights.

What part of the car is the laziest?
The wheels, because they are always tyred.

Why did the tomato blush?
It saw the salad dressing.

Why don't bikes stand up on their own?
They are two tyred.

How do you make a pop star out of a duck?
Put it in a microwave and its Bill Withers.

"Doctor, Doctor, think I am going deaf."
"What are the symptoms?"
"A yellow cartoon family on TV."

Knock! Knock!
Who's there?
Owls say.
Owls say who?
That's correct.

What did the stamp say to the envelope?
Stick with me and we'll go places.

What does an auctioneer know?
Lots.

Doctor: "Do the sleeping pills help?"
Patient: "No. Now I dream I don't sleep."

You were long in the Doctor's surgery?
I was the same size as I am now.

What do you call a woman with a sausage on her head?
Barbie.

Why couldn't the pirate play cards?
Because he was standing on the deck.

What did the laundryman say to the impatient
customer?
"Keep your shirt on."

As I stopped to pick a buttercup, I wondered:
"I wonder who owns this buttock and how did they
lose it?"

Why did the boy wear plimsolls on his head?
To try and jog his memory.

Who was the scariest dinosaur?
The Terror-dactyl.

What is the difference between a TV and a newspaper?
Have you ever tried swatting a fly with a TV?

What did one lift say to the other lift?
I think I'm coming down with something.

"Doctor, Doctor, I have strawberries on my head."
"I have some cream for that."

What do you call a woman with a radiator on her head?
Anita.

What is the difference between ammonia and
pneumonia?
One comes in a bottle, the other in chests.

Why was the belt arrested?
Because it held up some trousers.

Why was everyone so tired on April 1st?
They had just finished a March of 31 days.

Where do all the pencils come from?
Pennsylvania.

Knock! Knock!
Who's there?
Noah.
Noah who?
Noah good place to go and eat?

Which hand is it better to write with?
Neither, it's best to write with a pen.

Why can't your nose be 12 inches long?
Because then it would be a foot.

How many atheists does it take to change a lightbulb?
None. They have never seen the light in the first place.

Why is a calendar popular?
Because it has a lot of dates.

Confucius say he who behave like ass will be butt of
jokers.

Why did Mickey Mouse go into outer space?
To find Pluto.

What is overlooked by even the most careful person?
Their nose.

Did you hear about the robbery last night?
Two clothes pegs held up a pair of trousers.

Why was the driver arrested?
For cutting up a side street.

What do you call a woman with no arms or legs on a wire fence?
Barb.

How long should an elephant's legs be?
Long enough to reach the ground.

"Doctor, Doctor, my hands won't stop shaking."
"Do you drink a lot?"
"No I mostly spill it."

Did you hear about the magic tractor?
It turned into a field.

How do you cure a headache?
Put your head through a window and the pane will just disappear.

BATTY BOOKS (2)

From one AD to the present day by Anne O'Domini
Garden weeds by Dan D Lyon
Give to the poor by Robin Deritch
Gymnastics by Horace Zontlebars
Harbouring a Chinese fugitive by Hu Yu Hai Ding
History of rag & bone men by Orson Cart
Horrible hernia by Won Hung Low
Horse riding for fun by G G Canters
Last minute plans by Justin Time
Laying carpets by Walter Wall
Losing my mind by C Nility
Making money by Ivor Fortune
Making more money by Millie O'Naire
Messing around by Jo King
Moving abroad by Emma Grate
Moving house by Ivor Newhome
On parole by Freda Convict
On the rocks by Mandy Lifeboat
On the wet sand by C Shaw
Pachyderms by L E Fant
Pants on the carpet by Drew P Draws
Parachute jumping for beginners by Willie Maykit
Pavements by C Ment
Practical jokes by Paul D Utherwan

What kind of car does Mickey Mouse's wife drive?
A Minnie van.

Why did Julius Caesar buy charcoal sticks?
He wanted to Mark Antony.

Why don't traffic lights ever go swimming?
Because they take too long to change.

Did you hear that the police were called to a
kindergarten?
A three-year-old was resisting a rest.

What do you call a woman in the middle of a tennis
court?
Annette.

Did you hear about the tax loophole?
It became a noose.

Why did the man run around his bed?
To catch up on his sleep.

Knock! Knock!
Who's there?
Paris.
Paris who?
Paris a score you want to beat in golf.

Did you hear about the man who stood behind a horse?
He got a kick out of it.

What do you call a confused panda at the teddy bear's picnic?
Bamboozled.

How many elephants does it take to change a lightbulb?
One. But it has to stand on a trunk to do it.

How do you ask a man with no arms and no legs the time?
"Got the time on yer, Cock?"

A man crashed between to semi-detached houses.
In one house lived the Balls family and in the other, the Smiths.
Luckily he was dragged from the wreckage by the Smiths.

Why did the Siamese twins move from the USA to the UK?
So that the other one could learn to drive as well.

Why was the map gesticulating?
It was an animated map.

Waiter! Waiter!
There's a dead fly in my soup.
Yes sir, it looks like it has committed insecticide.

What do you have when you have a green ball in one hand and a green ball in the other?
The Jolly Green Giant's undivided attention.

What ties do pigs wear to work?
Pigs ties.

What do you call a really old ant?
Antique.

First stupid man: "Look! A dead bird."
Second stupid man (looking up): "Where?"

Teacher: "What is 2n plus 2n?"
Student: "I don't know. It's 4n to me."

How does Batman's mother call him to dinner?
Dinner, Dinner, Dinner, Dinner, Batman! (Sung to the 1960's TV theme tune)

What did the man say after getting married to two different women?
That's bigamy.

What washes up on very small beaches?
Microwaves.

What do you call a bear with no ears?
B.

"Doctor, Doctor, when I stand up quickly I see Mickey Mouse."
"You are having a Disney spell."

There was an old man from Peru,
Who dreamed he was eating a poo.
He awoke in the night
With a terrible fright,
And found it was perfectly true.

Why did the fisherman put peanut butter into the sea?
To go with the jellyfish.

What are stolen sweets called?
Hot chocolate.

What kind of nuts always seems to have a cold?
Cashews.

I say, I say, I say.
My wife's just been studying marine science in the
Indian Ocean.
Seychelles?
No, just the molluscs.

Knock! Knock!
Who's there?
Nile.
Nile who?
Nile down and I'll tell you.

A successful diet is the triumph of mind over platter.

What is big, white, and furry and always points North?
A polar bearing.

Why are poets poor?
Because rhyme doesn't pay.

What do you call two ants that run away to get
married?
Antelopes.

What is green, lives in the vegetable patch and sings?
Elvis Parsley.

Why did the banana go to the doctor?
Because it wasn't peeling well.

Why won't you starve in a desert?
Because of all the sand which is there.

Waiter! Waiter!
There's a dead fly in my soup!
Yes sir, the hot water kills them.

What do nuts put on their feet?
Cashews.

How do you make a walnut laugh?
Crack it up.

What's a Greek urn?
About ten euros an hour.

What bread to do elves use for sandwiches?
Shortbread.

Did you hear about the driver who swerved to avoid a
box of nails?
He was arrested for tacks evasion.

What do you call a man with motorbike helmet on his head?
Anything you like.

Why shouldn't you tell a secret on a farm?
Because the potatoes have eyes and the corn has ears.

What is a pretzel's favourite dance?
The Twist.

"Doctor, Doctor, I think I am invisible."
"I can't see you now."

What is the favourite fruit of twins?
Pears.

Knock! Knock!
Who's there?
Qatar.
Qatar who?
Qatar is not what you get when you have a cold.

If a crocodile makes shoes, what does a banana make?
Slippers.

What do you call a peanut in a spacesuit?
An astronut.

Noah's Ark – made of wood.
Joan of Arc – Maid of Orleans.

Did you hear about the stupid jellyfish?
It set.

What do you give to a sick lemon?
Lemon aid.

What is brown and chunky in space?
A cocoanaut.

How do you make a milk shake?
Scare it.

What kind of keys do kids like to carry?
Cookies.

"What have you been doing today?" says the king to his
knight.
"I have been pillaging on your behalf and burning the
villages of your enemies in the north, sire."
"But I don't have any enemies in the north."
"Well you do now, my liege."

What do you do if you see a spaceman?
Like, you park in it, man.

What cheese is made backwards?
Edam.

What did the big flower say to the little flower?
Alright petal?

What do you call a man on a wall?
Art.

What did Mars say to Saturn?
Give me a ring sometime.

What did the big flower say to the small flower?
What's up bud?

Where does seaweed go to look for a job?
The kelp wanted section.

"Doctor, Doctor, I want to spray myself with gold paint."
"Relax, you've just got a gilt complex."

How can you tell that a tree is a dogwood tree?
By its bark.

What did the little tree say to the big tree?
Leaf me alone.

What do you get if your pour boiling water down a rabbit hole?
Hot cross bunnies.

Waiter! Waiter!
This coffee tastes like mud!
I'm not surprised, sir, it was ground only a few minutes ago.

Did you hear the joke about the maize field?
It's a corny one.

What do barristers wear to court?
Lawsuits.

Knock! Knock!
Who's there?
Nana.
Nana who?
Nana your business.

Did you hear about the corn field?
It's amaizing.

No matter how much you push the envelope, it'll still be stationery.

What do you call a woman with a spring on her head?
April.

Why did the pine tree get into trouble?
Because it was being knotty.

Why did Father Christmas' helper see the doctor?
Because he had low elf esteem.

What happens if you eat yeast and shoe polish?
Every morning you'll rise and shine!

Who is the trendiest animal at an African watering hole?
The hip-opotamus.

How many mice does it take to screw in a lightbulb?
Two. But the trick is getting them in there.

"Doctor, Doctor, I see spots before my eyes."
"Have you seen an optician?"
"No, just spots."

Did you hear about the salad bowl race?
The lettuce was a head and the tomato was trying to ketchup.

What do you get from a pampered cow?
Spoiled milk.

Why didn't the map grids go to the punk disco?
Because they were all squares.

What did one pencil say to the other pencil?
"You look sharp."

What did bacon say to the tomato?
Lettuce get together.

What is the most hardworking part of the eye?
The pupil.

A will is a dead giveaway.

Why was the Pharaoh boastful?
Because he Sphinx he's the best.

What do you call a man with a raincoat?
Mac.

What do you call a man with a large raincoat?
Big Mac.

What do you call a man with two raincoats?
Max.

What do you call a man with two raincoats in a
cemetery?
Max Bygraves.

Knock! Knock!
Who's there?
Rabbit.
Rabbit who?
Rabbit up neatly, it's a present.

Waiter! Waiter!
There's a dead beetle in my soup.
Yes sir, they're not very good swimmers.

How do you make a Kleenex dance?
Blow a boogey into it.

Confucius say man kicked in balls left holding bag.

What do you get when you cross fish and an elephant?
Swimming trunks.

Where do bees go to the bathroom?
At the BP station.

What is the definition of a harp?
A piano after tax.

How do you get down from an elephant?
You don't. You get down from a duck.

Who drives their customers away to make money?
Taxi drivers.

How do you shoot a killer bee?
With a b-b gun.

What do you call an Indian cloakroom attendant?
Mahatma coat.

What happened to the dog that swallowed a firefly?
It barked with de-light.

Why are frogs so happy?
They eat whatever bugs them

What do you get when you cross a cow and a duck?
Milk and quackers.

When do astronauts eat their sandwiches?
Launch time.

Did you hear about the unlucky gambler?
He bet on a horse at ten-to-one and it came in at a
quarter-past-four.

What vegetables don't sailors like?
Leeks.

Drill-sergeant to army private: "I didn't see you at
camouflage practice last night. Well done."

What do you call a donkey with three legs?
Wonkey.

Did you hear about the paper shop?
It blew away.

Two nuns in a car when a vampire drops onto their
bonnet.
"Quick!" says the fist nun. "Show him your cross."
So the second nun opens the door and shouts "Get off
my bonnet this instant. I've just had it cleaned and if
you damage anything you can pay for it!"

Have you heard about the block of flats?
It's a tall story.

What do you call a parrot in a raincoat?
Polly-unsaturated.

Why did the tomato go out with the prune?
Because it couldn't find a date.

Why do fungi have to pay more on a bus?
They take up too mushroom.

Did you hear about the man who slept like a log?
He woke up in the fireplace

"Doctor, Doctor, can you give me something for this wind?"
"How about a kite?"

When is the moon the heaviest?
When it's full.

Jokes about German sausage are the wurst.

What did the beaver say to the tree?
It's been nice gnawing you.

What do you call a man with no arms or legs in a pile of leaves?
Russell.

Why did the grass go to the doctor?
It was feeling a bit green.

What month to trees hate?
Septimber.

What tree fits into your hand?
A palm tree.

What do you call a woman with the Titanic on her head?
Mandy Lifeboats.

Acupuncture - a jab well done.

What did the leopard say after eating his owner?
That hit the spot.

Why is England the wettest country?
Because the queen has reigned there for years.

What has eight legs and eight eyes?
Eight pirates.

Is dreaming in colour just a pigment of your imagination?

How many economists does it take to change a lightbulb?
None. Market forces have already caused the change.

Why do fish live in salt water?
Because pepper makes them sneeze.

"Doctor, Doctor, I think I am a twig!"
"Don't snap!"

Why did the man put his money in the freezer?
He wanted cold, hard cash.

What do you get when you cross a snowman with a
vampire?
Frostbite.

Knock! Knock!
Who's there?
Dozen.
Dozen who?
Dozen anyone want to let me in?

What is the best day to go to the beach?
Sunday.

What bow can't you tie?
A rainbow.

What season is the best for jumping on a trampoline?
Spring time.

I say, I say, I say.
My wife's just been in an accident on a volcano.
Krakatoa?
No. She broke her leg.

What do you call a bear with no paw?
Rupert the bastard.

Where did the computer go to dance?
To a disc-o.

Waiter! Waiter!
This coffee is way too strong!
You may be old and weak yourself one day.

Confucius say person hit by car feel run down.

What has one head, one foot and four legs?
A bed.

What is the difference between a school teacher and a train?
The teacher says spit your gum out, but a train says chew-chew.

Why does history keep repeating itself?
Because no-one in class was listening.

Roses are red,
Violets are blue,
I'm schizophrenic,
And so am I.

Why did the canary go to the hospital?
To get a tweetment.

What sound do porcupines make when they kiss?
"Ouch."

What do you call a detective from the reformation?
Martin Sleuther.

Why was stupid man looking for fast food on his friend?
Because his friend said dinner is on him.

Did you hear the joke about the roof?
Never mind, it's over your head!

Why didn't the skeleton go to the dance?
Because he had no-body to go with.

Knock! Knock!
Who's there?
Eureka.
Eureka who?
Eureka something, and it really pongs.

How can you eat an egg without breaking its shell?
Get someone else to break it.

What do you call a man with a rubber toe?
Roberto.

How did the cricket feel when he hurt his leg?
Unhoppy.

Why are pirates called pirates?
Because they arrrrr.

Did you hear about the Cockney fairy?
She though Christmas was a pine up the bum.

Did you hear about the soldier who survived mustard
gas and pepper spray?
He is a seasoned veteran.

What did the tree do when the bank closed?
It started a new branch.

"Doctor, Doctor, I am shrinking."
"Be a little patient."

A talking sheepdog got all the sheep into their pen. "All
40 accounted for," he said.
"But there's only 38 in there," replied the farmer
"I know, I rounded them up."

Did you hear the story about the peacock?
It's a beautiful tale.

Why is rain like a cat?
Because when it rains it purrs.

How can you tune into the solar system?
Use a sundial.

What do you call a vicar on a moped?
Rev.

Mary had a little lamb
You've heard this tale before –
But did you know she finished her plate
And had a little more?

What did one chemist say when a colleague threw
Sodium Chloride over him?
"Technically speaking, that's a salt."

Who steals from your bathroom?
A robber duck.

What is the difference between unlawful and illegal?
One is something which is against the law and the
other is a sick bird of prey.

How many dancers does it take to change a lightbulb?
A one, two, three, and.

A man goes into a pub and the barman says:
"we haven't seen you for a while."
The man replies: "I've been doing chores."
"What chores?" asks the barman.
"Thank you," replies the man. "I'll have a pint please."

How do mad men go through the forest?
They take the psycho path.

Where is it always 90 degrees, but never hot?
The Pole (north and south).

What do prisoners use to call each other?
Cell phones.

What do you call a man with no arms or legs on a doorstep?
Matt.

Waiter! Waiter!
There's a dead fly in my soup.
I thought it smelled slightly off.

Knock! Knock!
Who's there?
Doctor.
Doctor who?

Where do snowmen keep their money?
In snow banks.

What do you call a giant pile of kittens?
A meowntain.

What goes through towns, up & over hills, but doesn't move?
A road.

Why was there thunder and lightning in the lab?
The scientists were brainstorming.

Why did the man go out with a prune?
Because he couldn't find a date.

What did the little mountain say to the big mountain?
Hi Cliff.

"Doctor, Doctor, I've swallowed a shark fish bone."
"This is not time to choke."

What did Winnie the Pooh say to his agent?
Show me the honey.

What do Winnie the Pooh and Alfred the Great have in common?
The same middle name.

Why did the traffic light turn red?
It had to change in the middle of the street.

How do you make an octopus laugh?
With ten-tickles.

What starts with a P, ends with an E, and has a million letters in it?
Post Office.

What do you call a woman with my tortoise on her head?
Michelle.

What did the duvet say to the bed?
I've got you covered.

Why did Socrates like battered fish for tea?
Because it was fried in Greece.

Did you hear about the man who took a pencil to bed?
He wanted to draw the curtains.

How many books can you put in an empty backpack?
One. After that it isn't empty.

A new floor was put down in the play school.
It is called infant-tile.

"Doctor, Doctor, my snoring is keeping me awake."
"Have you tried sleeping in the other room?"

Knock! Knock!
Who's there?
Death.
Death wh …

Did you hear about the eye doctor on an Alaskan island?
He was an optical Aleutian.

What kind of button won't undo?
A tummy button.

How can a leopard change his spots?
Move to another place.

Why do ants eat most food in the summer?
They go to a lot of picnics

Where do cats got to get some culture?
The mewseum.

What kind of luggage to vultures take on planes?
Carrion.

How do you fix a short circuit?
Lengthen it.

What do you call a US oilman in a sauna?
Red.

Why is your nose in the middle of your face?
Because it is the scenter.

Did you hear about the dog who went to the flea
circus?
He stole the show.

A English cat called one, two, three challenged his
French cousin, called un, deux, trois, to a swimming
race across the Channel. One, two, three cat won
because un, deux, trois cat sank!

Corduroy pillows are making headlines.

Did you hear about the cheese factory explosion?
There was de brie everywhere.

"Doctor, Doctor, I think I am a goat."
"How long has this been going on?"
"Since I was a kid."

What is the saddest cheese?
Blue cheese.

Waiter! Waiter!
There's a fly in my soup.
Don't worry sir, the spider on your roll will eat it.

Did you hear about the boy who threw cheddar at
people?
It wasn't mature.

Why was the cheesemonger lopsided?
He only had one stilton.

What do you call a man with an amplifier on his head?
Mike.

What kind of cheese do horses like?
Mascarpone.

Knock! Knock!
Who's there?
Dakota.
Dakota who?
Dakota ma wearing is yours.

Why were the Dark Ages so called?
Because there were too many knights.

Did you hear about the man who tried to make clothes
from cheese?
It didn't work because fromage frays.

How do you shorten a bed?
Don't sleep long in it.

What do you call a hippie's wife?
Mississippi.

I say, I say, I say.
My wife's just been to a bad concert in the Far East.
Singapore?
Yes and so was the band.

What did the triangle say to the circle?
You are pointless.

Why do seagulls fly over the sea?
Because if they flew over the bay they would be bagels.

What day don't eggs like?
Fry day.

What do you call a man with a map on his head?
Miles.

What dog keeps the best time?
A watch dog.

What did the grape say when it got stepped on?
Nothing. It just let out a little wine.

What did the judge say when the skunk walked in the
court room?
Odour in the court.

What did the fish say when he swam into the wall?
"Dam!"

Confucius say man who sit on drawing pin get point.

An extraordinary fellow named Flynn
Was really remarkably thin
When he carried a pole
People said: "Bless my soul
We didn't know you had a twin."
Why don't skeletons fight each other?
They don't have the guts.

Is a book on voyeurism a peeping tome?

Why did the scientist go to the tanning salon?
Because he was a pale-ontologist.

Why was six wary of seven?
Because seven eight nine.

Why was the student's report wet?
It was below C level.

Waiter! Waiter!
There's a twig in my soup.
Yes, sir, we've got branches everywhere.

"Doctor, Doctor, I can't stop telling lies."
"I find that hard to believe."

What did the traffic light say to the car?
Don't look now, I'm changing.

What streets do ghosts haunt?
Dead ends.

"Our new vet seems very well qualified."
"Yes. He used to hold an important post at Battersea
Dogs Home."

Knock! Knock!
Who's there?
Cows say.
Cows say who?
No, cows say moo.

What do you call a cow that can play the piano?
A moosician.

What did the penny say to the other penny?
Let's change.

I say, I say, I say.
My wife's just had an accident in Slovenia.
Bled?
It wouldn't stop.

What did the cheese say to its reflection in the mirror?
Halloumi.

Why did the man with one hand cross the road?
To get to the second hand shop.

Why did the boy sprinkle sugar on his pillow before sleeping?
To have sweet dreams.

Doctor: "I have got some good news and some bad news."
Patient: "Give me the bad news, first."
Doctor: "You have only got 24 hours to live."
Patient: "What's the good news?"
Doctor: "I am having dinner with that beautiful nurse."

What do you call a man with a mat on his head?
Neil.

Why did the robber take a bath?
Because he wanted to make a clean getaway.

What did the judge say to the dentist?
Do you swear to pull the tooth, the whole tooth and nothing but the tooth.

Why did the boy tiptoe past the medicine cabinet?
So as not to wake the sleeping pills.

What do you get when you cross a fridge with a radio?
Cool Music.

What goes up when the rain comes down?
An umbrella.

"Doctor, Doctor, I have a lettuce leaf growing out of
my bottom – is it serious?"
"I'm afraid it is just the tip of the iceberg."

What do you call a line of rabbits hopping backwards?
A receding hare line.

How does one cheese compliment another?
Looking gouda…

Why don't you see giraffes in primary school?
Because they're all in high school.

Could alphabet soup left on a stove spell disaster?

I hired an odd-job man to do 8 jobs for me.
When I got back, he'd only done jobs 1, 3 5 and 7 on
the list.

Which is the longest word in the dictionary?
Smiles. There is a mile between each S.

Which month do soldiers hate most?
March.

Why did Goofy put a clock under his desk?
Because he wanted to work over-time.

Knock! Knock!
Who's there?
Europe.
Europe who?
No, you are.

Why did the boy throw the clock out of the window?
Because he wanted to see time fly.

Waiter! Waiter!
There's a fly in my soup.
I thought chef used them all in the raisin bread.

Dancing cheek-to-cheek is a form of floor play.

When do you stop at green and go at red?
When you're eating a watermelon.

What kind of tree do maths teachers like best?
Geometry.

How did the farmer mend his trousers?
With cabbage patches.

What do you call a stag with no eyes?
No idea.

What do you call a stag with no eyes or legs?
Still no idea.

Why did the man lose his job at the orange juice
factory?
He couldn't concentrate.

How did the Vikings communicate when they were at
sea?
Norse code.

How do you repair a broken tomato?
Tomato paste.

Why did the strawberry want to help?
Because his family were in a jam.

What was the Cat in the Hat looking for in the toilet?
For thing one and thing two.

What kind of money do elves use?
Jingle bills.

What did the hamburger name his daughter?
Patty.

"Doctor, Doctor, I think I have amnesia."
"Go home and forget about it."

What kind of egg did the bad chicken lay?
A devilled egg.

What do you call a person with no body, just a nose?
Nobody knows.

What kind of key opens the door at Christmas?
A turkey.

Why did the biscuit go to the hospital?
He felt crummy.

Why did the teacher have his eyes crossed?
He couldn't control her pupils.

Knock! Knock!
Who's there?
Chopin.
Chopin who?
Chopin at the supermarket, back soon.

What can you serve but never eat?
A tennis ball.

What kind of shoes do spies wear?
Sneakers.

Why did the footballer bring string to the game?
So he could tie the score.

What did the alien say to the garden?
Take me to your weeder.

Have you heard the joke about the butter?
I can't tell you, you might spread it.

Confucius say he who take laxative and sleeping pill on same night wake up in mess.

How do sportsmen stay cool?
They stand next to their fans.

Why was the maths textbook sad?
Because it had too many problems.

"Doctor, Doctor, what is the quickest way to get to hospital."
"Lie down in the middle of the road."

What do you call lazy kangaroo babies?
Pouch potatoes.

How many management consultants does it take to change a lightbulb?
None. They never get past the feasibility study.

What is an astronaut's favourite place on a computer?
The space bar.

What exam do all witches have to pass?
A spelling test.

Why did the boy eat his homework?
Because his teacher said it was a piece of cake.

Why is Basketball so messy?
Because you dribble on the floor.

Why can't you argue with angry dolphins?
They are talking at cross porpoises.

What is always in the corner but can move all round the world?
A postage stamp.

Did you hear about the man locked in a kiln?
He was fired.

How do you communicate with fish?
Drop them a line.

What do you call a monk's sin?
Nun.

Where do sheep get haircuts?
The baa baa shop.

Did you hear about the book about anti-gravity?
You can't put it down.

What is a cat's favourite cereal?
Mice Crispies.

Why can't leopards play hide and seek?
Because they are always spotted.

What do you call a hippie in Turkey?
Otto, man.

Did you hear about the magician's family who he
turned into a three piece suite?
The report from the hospital says they're comfortable.

What do you give a dog with a fever?
Mustard, it's the best thing for a hot dog.

What do you get when you cross a cat with a lemon?
A sour puss.

What was the sick horse suffering from?
Hay fever.

What do you call a sceptic cat?
Puss.

Why was the lentil embarrassed?
Because it saw the chick pea.

How do you make a Maltese Cross?
Step on his toe.

If runners get athletes foot do fighter pilots get
missile-toe.

How do you make a garden laugh?
Hoe, hoe, hoe.

What do you get if you cross a Martian with a kangaroo?
A marsupial.

Why was the fishmonger mean?
Because his job made him selfish.

Who delivers puppies if the vet is busy?
A mid-woof.

Did you hear about the man who made clown shoes?
It was no small feat.

How do you get an astronaut's baby to sleep?
Rocket.

What did one vegetarian say to the other vegetarian?
We have to stop meating like this.

Why does a graveyard have a wall around it?
Because people are dying to get in.

A small boy lost his dad so asked a policeman for help.
"What's he like?" asked the copper.
"Beer and football," he replied.

Why do birds fly south for the winter?
It is too far to walk.

If you can think of a better fish pun, please let minnow.

What kind of key opens a banana?
A monkey.

How do you know that carrots are good for your
eyesight?
Have you ever seen a rabbit wearing glasses?

Knock! Knock!
Who's there?
Cook.
Cook who?
Who are you calling cuckoo?

Why do hummingbirds hum?
They don't know the words.

Why are some fish at the bottom of the ocean?
Because they dropped out of school.

What do you call a pig that knows karate?
Pork chop.

What is a mathematician's favourite dessert?
Pi.

"Doctor, Doctor, I get a pain in my eye when I drink a
cup of tea."
"Try taking the teaspoon out of your cup."

How can you tell the old rabbits from the young ones?
Look for the grey hares.

What goes up and down but doesn't move?
The temperature.

What happened to the wooden car with wooden wheels
and wooden engine?
It wooden go.

How do you get two whales in a mini?
Over the Severn Bridge.

Which weighs more, a ton of feathers or a ton of
bricks?
Neither, they both weigh a ton.

Where do bulls get their messages?
On a bull-etin board.

What runs but can't walk?
A tap.

What do you call an Irishman with double glazing on his
head?
Paddy O'Doors.

"Doctor, Doctor, I've only got 59 seconds to live?"
"Wait a minute, please."

When does the Chinese man go to the dentist?
Tooth-hurty.

When does the Chinese man's brother go to the dentist?
Tooth-hurty-too.

What kind of bed does a mermaid sleep in?
A water bed.

What do you call a man buried under soil for a
century?
Pete.

Knock! Knock!
Who's there?
Francis.
Francis who?
France is a country in Europe.

What kind of jokes do you make in the shower?
Clean ones.

What kind of biscuits do firemen like with their cheese?
Firecrackers.

I say, I say, I say.
My wife's just gone to the West Indies.
Jamaica?
No, she went of her own accord.

What kind of tea did the American colonists want?
Liberty.

Why did the barber win the race?
He took a short cut.

Waiter! Waiter!
There's a small slug on this lettuce.
Would you like me to get you a bigger one?

What is taken before you get it?
Your picture.

Why did the tree go to the dentist?
To get a root canal.

Roses are red,
Violets are blue,
I have a short term memory.

What is it called when a cat wins a dog show?
A cat-has-trophy.

What can go up a chimney down, but can't go down
a chimney up?
An umbrella.

What do you call a man pouring water into a jug?
Phil.

What's the difference between Ms and Mrs?
Mr.

Why did Father Christmas tell off one of his elves?
Because he was goblin his Christmas dinner.

Where does a tree store their stuff?
In the trunk.

What did the nose say to the finger?
Stop picking on me.

How many jugglers does it take to change a lightbulb?
One. But they need at least three bulbs.

What did one plate say to the other?
This dinner is on me.

I wondered why the cricket ball was getting bigger.
Then it hit me.

Who cleans the bottom of the ocean?
A mer-maid

What do you call a kidney that paints?
Piss artist.

What lies at the bottom of the sea and shakes?
A nervous wreck.

Knock! Knock!
Who's there?
Genoa.
Genoa who?
Genoa, cos I've never seen her before in my life.

Patient: "I haven't spoken to my wife for 20 years."
Doctor: "Why on earth not, man?"
Patient: "I didn't like to interrupt her."

Where do crayons go on holiday?
Pennsylvania.

What do you call a man with a plank on his head?
Edward.

What do you call a man with two planks on his head?
Edward Wood.

What do you call a man with three planks on his head?
Edward Woodward.

What do you call a man with four planks on his head?
I don't know – but Edward Woodward would.

What is heavy forward but not backward?
Ton.

What do you get when you plant kisses?
Tu-lips.

What pet makes the loudest noise?
A trumpet.

Why did the girl bring lipstick and eye shadow to
school?
She had a make-up exam.

What is a bubble's least favourite drink?
Soda pop.

Confucius say he who sneezes without tissue take
matters into own hands.

Name a city where no one goes?
Electricity.

What do you call a woman setting fire to her phone
bill?
Bernadette.

Where did Montezuma go to college?
Az Tech.

What is the difference between a cat and a frog?
A cat has nine lives, but a frog croaks every night.

Knock! Knock!
Who's there?
Canoe.
Canoe who?
Canoe come to my party?

Why can't you trust atoms?
They make up everything.

Where does bad light go?
To prism.

I am a dog
And you are a flower
I lift my leg up
And give you a shower.

If frozen water is iced water and if frozen lemonade is
iced lemonade – what is frozen ink?
Iced ink.

What is the definition of a transistor?
A nun after a sex change.

What did the sea say to the shore?
Nothing, it just waved.

What did the angry physics teacher say when he
wanted to fight two teachers?
"Let me atom."

Two peanuts were walking down the street.
One was a salted.

If you had eight apples in one hand and five apples in
the other, what would you have?
Really big hands.

"Doctor, Doctor, I can't get to sleep."
"Lie on the edge of your bed and you'll soon drop off."

Two biscuits were run over.
Crumbs!

Did you hear about the man who dreamt that he was a car silencer?
He woke up exhausted.

For how much did the man sell his used batteries?
Nothing, they were free of charge.

Did you hear about the man we wouldn't enter his house?
His case was outstanding.

Pencil sharpeners have a tough life.
They live off tips.

Dijon vu.
It's the same mustard as before.

Have you heard about the broken pencil?
It is pointless.

What do you call a dinosaur with only one eye?
D'you-think-he-saw-us.

What do you call a dinosaur with only one eye and a dog?
D'you-think-he-saw-us-rex.

A LIST OF NATIONS (2)

Hallucination	- full of crazies
Hibernation	- where winters fly by
Illumination	- a place for the very bright
Imagination	- inhabited by the fanciful
Impersonation	- inhabited by the overly dramatic
Incarnation	- where people always drive
Inclination	- inhabited by those interested in learning
Indignation	- for those filled with righteous anger
Insubordination	- full or disrespectful people
Machination	- a place full of schemers
Nomination	- where people are highly political
Origination	- where life began
Oxygenation	- for bubbly personalities
Pagination	- inhabitation by numbers
Peregrination	- where the foot weary travellers live
Pollination	- inhabited by parrots
Procrastination	- about whom I'll let you know in my next book
Profanation	- *@#!~?
Resignation	- inhabited by those who accept their fate
Subordination	- for the subservient in life
Termination	- where life has ceased to be
Trepanation	- for those with a hole in their skull
Urination	- a bog standard place
Vaccination	- where healthy people live

Knock! Knock!
Who's there?
Hungary.
Hungary who?
Hungary and homeless, please give generously.

Silence is golden.
Duct tape is silver.

How did Bob Marley like his doughnuts?
Wi' jam in.

What did Bob Marley say to his girlfriend when he
gave her a doughnut?
"I hope you like jam in too."

Did you hear about the man who tried to catch some fog?
He mist.

Change is hard.
Have you ever tried to bend a coin?

If money doesn't grow on trees why do banks have
branches?

Waiter! Waiter!
There's a fly in my soup.
Please be quiet, sir, or they'll all want one.

Did you hear about the man who was fired from the
calendar factory?
It was for taking a day off.

Why did the origami teacher hate his job?
There was too much paperwork.

What do elves learn at school?
The elfabet.

Teacher: "What came after the stone and bronze age?"
Pupil: "The sausage?"

I say, I say, I say.
My wife's just been to the botanical gardens.
Kew?
Yes. She had to wait for ages.

What do you call a man with a receipt on his head?
Bill.

Why do bees have sticky hair?
Because they use honeycombs.

Why do cows wear bells?
Because their horns don't work.

Knock! Knock!
Who's there?
Hatch.
Hatch who?
Bless you.

"Doctor, Doctor, I my feet smell and my nose runs."
"Are you upside down?"

What is black and white, black and white, black and white?
A penguin rolling down a hill.

What did the snail say when he was riding on a tortoise's shell?
Wheeeee.

What is brown and sticky?
A stick.

What do parents like at the fun-fair?
The married-go-round!

Where do cows go on Friday night?
To the moovies.

What do you call a man with a spade in his head?
Doug.

What do you call a man without a spade in his head?
Douglas.

Did you hear about the butcher who sat on his bacon slicer?
He got a little behind in his orders.

Where did the king keep his armies?
Up his sleevies.

Why did King Arthur have a round table?
So he couldn't be cornered.

Where do library books like to sleep?
Under their covers.

Why can't a tyrannosaurus rex clap?
It's extinct.

Knock! Knock!
Who's there?
Canada.
Canada who?
Can Ada come and play please mum?

Girl: "Why is your nose so swollen?"
Boy: "I was smelling a brose."
Girl: "There is no B in rose."
Boy: "There was in this one."

What do deer read in the morning?
A moosepaper.

What do you call a Chinese woman with a Kenwood
on her head?
Blenda.

What does a piece of toast wear to bed?
His py-jam-as.

"Doctor, Doctor, I've broken my leg in two places."
"Don't go back to either of them again, then."

Why did the bee get married?
Because he found his honey.

What sound does a cow with no lips make?
Oooo.

What is invisible and smells of bananas?
A monkey's burp.

What did the daddy buffalo say to his son when he
went to school?
Bison.

What did one teddy bear say to the other teddy bear?
I'm stuffed.

Why don't you ever see elephants playing hide and
seek?
Because they're really good at it.

What do you call a man with no arms or legs in a pool?
Bob.

What do you call a man with no arms or legs trying to
get out of a pool?
Bob Hope.

Where do cows like to go shopping?
Moo York.

How do you catch a unique rabbit?
Unique up on it.

And do you know how you catch a tame rabbit?
Tame way.

What do you get if you cross a farm animal with a mapmaker?
A cow-tographer.

"Doctor, Doctor, I keep having déjà-vu."
"You said that to me yesterday."

What cheese do you use to get a bear out of a tree?
Come-on-bear (camembert).

What do pigs use for medicine?
Oinkment.

Why does Tarzan where plastic pants?
To keep his nuts jungle fresh.

What is yellow, smells of almonds and swings through the jungle?
Tarzipan.

Does the name Pavlov ring a bell?

Why is Ireland such a rich country?
Because its capital is always Dublin.

How do elephants hide in a cherry tree?
They paint their toenails red.

How did the giraffe get squashed?
Biting cherries from a tree.

Doctor: "You have a bladder infection."
Patient: "Is it serious?"
Doctor: "Yes. Urine trouble."

Knock! Knock!
Who's there?
Bucharest.
Bucharest who?
Bucharest at my hotel and you won't regret it.

Why are an elephant's feet wrinkled?
To give the ants a 50:50 chance.

Confucius say man who walk through airport turnstile sideways going to Bangkok.

Why did the turtle cross the road?
To get to the shell station.

What did the dinosaur die after taking a bath?
Because he was ex-stinked.

When is a black bird not a black bird?
When it's a crow.

Why didn't true north go out with magnetic north?
She didn't like his bearing.

How do bees get to school?
On the school buzz.

What makes witches fall down?
A dizzy spell.

Where does Friday come before Monday?
In a dictionary.

What is black when clean, and white when dirty?
A blackboard.

Which driver has no arms or legs?
A screwdriver.

"Doctor, Doctor, I my eyesight is getting worse."
"This is a fish shop."

What do you call a failed lion tamer?
Claude.

What do you call a king who is only 12 inches tall?
A ruler.

What do you call secret agents at Christmas?
Mince pies.

Waiter! Waiter!
There's a mosquito in my soup.
Don't worry, it doesn't have a big appetite.

Which is the fastest runner - hot or cold water?
Hot, because you can catch cold.

What did one hair say to the other hair?
It takes two to tangle.

Why would Snow White make a great judge?
Because she was the fairest in the land.

What kind of underwear to barristers wear?
Legal briefs.

How many Elvis impersonators does it take to change
a lightbulb?
One for the money, two for the show, three to get ready
...

A swimmer whose clothing was strewed,
By winds that left her quite nude.
Saw a man come along,
And unless I am quite wrong,
You thought this was going to be rude.

Why didn't the boy take the bus home?
Because he thought his mother would make him take it
back.

What is the difference between a train driver and a teacher?
One minds the train, the other trains the mind.

What do you call a South African with pork chop on his head?
Brai.

What did the ceiling say to light?
You're the highlight of my life.

What is black and white and red all over?
An embarrassed mime artist.

Knock! Knock!
Who's there?
Henrietta.
Henrietta who?
Henrietta worm in his apple.

What did the mop say to the bucket?
You are looking pale today.

What sound do you get if you cross a clock with a maths teacher?
Arithmatic.

Who was the largest between Mr. Bigger, his wife, or their son?
Their son – he was just a little Bigger.

"Doctor, Doctor, is it true that exercise kills germs?"
"Possibly, but I don't know how to get them to do it."

Why did the boy take a ruler to bed?
To see how long he slept.

Why did the melon jump into the lake?
It wanted to be a watermelon.

What do you call a woman with one leg either side of a stream?
Bridgette.

What goes under your feet and over your head?
A skipping rope.

Why did the scientist remove his doorbell?
He wanted to win the no-bell prize!

I say, I say, I say.
My wife's just been to the Indian coast.
Goa?
I'll say!

What do you get when you cross a cowboy with a mapmaker?
A cow-tographer.

What did one tooth say to the other tooth?
The dentist is taking me out tonight.

What did the lawyer name his daughter?
Sue.

What has a head but no body?
A nail.

What do you call a man with an oil rig on his head?
Derek.

What do a baker and a millionaire have in common?
They are both have lots of dough.

Man in the audience: "How did you do that trick?"
Magician: "If I tell you, I'm afraid I'll have to kill you."
Man: "OK. Why don't you just tell my wife?"

Why did the gardener plant his money?
He wanted his soil to be rich.

Why did the banana split?
Because it saw the ginger snap.

Who invented King Arthur's round table?
Sir Circumference.

Knock! Knock!
Who's there?
Wallet.
Wallet who?
Walletsa one for the money, two for the show.

Why was the man fired from the car assembly line?
He was caught taking a brake.

Who are the most considerate school teachers?
Play school teachers, because they can make little things count.

What letter can you drink?
T.

What do you call a man with a large blue-black-yellow mark on his head?
Bruce.

What happened when the monster ate the electric pylon?
It was in shock for a week.

What do sea monsters eat for lunch?
Fish and ships.

"Doctor, Doctor, I think I am a moth."
"You should see a psychiatrist not me."
"I was on the way but your light was on."

How many lawyers does it take to change a lightbulb?
How many can you afford?

When is a car not a car?
When it turns into a garage.

What is always hot in the fridge?
Chili.

Confucius say he who eat prunes get good run for money.

Which archeologist works for Scotland Yard?
Sherlock Bones.

Why was the doctor so cross on holiday?
Because he had no patients.

England doesn't have a kidney bank.
It does have a Liverpool.

How did the man who discovered electricity feel?
Shocked.

If you drop a white hat into the Red Sea, what does it become?
Wet.

Where do elves go to get fit?
An elf farm.

What balls do dragons use for soccer?
Fireballs.

Where do all the letters sleep?
The alphabed.

What do you call a sad cup of coffee?
Depresso.

What has a bed that no one can sleep in?
A river.

Waiter! Waiter!
There's a fly in my soup.
Please don't worry sir, it is actually just a piece of dirt.

What is really in the middle of nowhere?
The letter H.

Knock! Knock!
Who's there?
Witches.
Witches who?
Witches the way to my house please?

"Doctor, Doctor, I feel like a pony."
"You are just a little hoarse."

Did you hear about the wild horses who fell in love?
It was a case of unbridled passion.

Which candles burn longer, bee's wax or tallow?
Neither, they all burn shorter.

What can you hold without using your hands?
Your breath.

Did you hear about the race between a piece of lettuce,
an egg and a tap?
The lettuce came in ahead, the egg got beaten, but the
tap is still running.

A calendar's days are numbered.

What was the Queen's father called?
The King.

What is only a small box but can weigh over a hundred pounds?
Scales.

Why did Columbus cross the ocean?
To get to the other tide.

What has lots of holes but still holds water?
A sponge.

When is a door not a door?
When it's ajar.

A sausage and bacon rasher were sizzling in a pan when the sausage says: "Wow, it's hot in here!"
The bacon rasher says: "Hey, a talking sausage."

How can two babies be born on the same day, in the same year, to the same parents, but not be twins?
They are triplets.

What do you call a cow that just had a baby?
De-calf-inated.

How many civil servants does it take to change a lightbulb?
45. One to do the work and the rest to do the paperwork.

Why don't honest people need beds?
They don't lie.

What did the boat say to the pier?
What's up, dock?

Why did the cucumber call for help?
It was in a pickle.

Doctor: "You have only 24 hours to live."
Patient: "What's the good news?"
Doctor: "You have lost your short term memory."
Patient: "Thank goodness, I thought you were going
tell me I had only a short time to live."

What runs around a field without moving?
A fence.

Knock! Knock!
Who's there?
Wilma.
Wilma who?
Wilma tea be ready soon?

What did the envelope say when it was licked?
Nothing, it was shut up.

Why are envelopes so haughty?
They are made to be stuck up.

What do you call a rabbit with fleas?
Bugs Bunny.

Roses are grey,
Violets are grey,
Everything's grey.
I must be colour blind.

What does a race winner lose?
His breath.

Why didn't the owl take his girlfriend out in the rain?
It was too wet to woo.

"Doctor, Doctor, I think I'm a snooker ball."
"Get to the end of the cue."

What kind of table has no legs?
A multiplication table.

How many insects does it take to fill a flat?
Ten ants.

What band doesn't play music?
A rubber band.

Why was the reporter obsessed with the ice cream tub?
He wanted a scoop.

Why is longitude smarter than latitude?
It has 360 degrees.

I say, I say, I say.
My wife's just gone mad in Venezuela.
Caracas?
Yes, completely doolally.

What do you call a sleeping bull?
A bulldozer.

What is 182 feet tall and made out of ham, cheese and tomato?
The leaning tower of pizza.

Who is the richest between the butcher, the baker and the candlestick maker?
The baker, because he has lots of dough.

Knock! Knock!
Who's there?
Wooden shoe.
Wooden shoe who?
Wooden shoe like to know.

What is the difference between a fly and superman?
Superman can fly, but a fly cannot superman.

What do you get if you eat a prune pizza?
Pizzeria.

What room can you not go into?
A mushroom.

What did the candle say to the other candle?
I'm going out tonight.

What is a baby's motto?
If at first you don't succeed, cry and cry again!

What is a pirate's favourite food?
Chips ahoy.

Why did James Bond stay in bed?
Because he was under cover.

A piece of frazzled string went into a pub and the
barman asks: "Are you a piece of string?"
"No," it replies, "I'm a frayed knot."

What kind of dinners do maths teachers eat?
Square meals.

"Doctor, Doctor, I feel like a packet of cheese biscuits."
"You're crackers."

What do you call a Welshman with a biscuit on his
head?
Dai Gestive.

What is a royal pardon?
It's what the queen says after she burps.

What did the chestnut say to the walnut?
Nothing. Nuts can't talk.

What is the best parting gift?
A comb.

Why did the journalist go to the ice cream parlor?
To get a scoop.

What is the fastest country in the world?
Russia.

What goes on and on and has an 'i' in the middle?
An onion.

What kind of jam can you not eat?
A traffic jam.

Doctor: "I have got some good news and some bad news for you."
Patient: "Give me the bad news, first."
Doctor: "I'll need to stitch that cut."
Patient: "I can do that, thanks."
Doctor: "Suture self."

Did you hear about the man who had a photographic memory?
It never developed.

What is a tornado's favorite game?
Twister.

Knock! Knock!
Who's there?
Will.
Will who?
Will you please just open the door?

Where does a cruise ship go when it is ill?
To the dock tour.

What do you call a woman with a bunch of holly on her
head?
Carol.

What did the green grape say to the purple grape?
"Breathe, you fool."

What did the pirate say on his 80th birthday?
"Aye-matey."

Why did the man turn down the mirror polishing job?
He couldn't see himself doing it.

How do snails fight?
They slug it out.

Waiter! Waiter!
There's a flea in my soup.
Don't worry sir, it isn't deep enough for it to drown.

What did the policeman say to his stomach?
You are under a vest.

What is a specimen?
An Italian astronaut.

What is big, grey and doesn't matter?
An irrelephant.

Confucius say man with one chopstick go hungry.

Why do the French eat snails?
Because they don't like fast food.

Why was longitude hot?
Because it was 360 degrees.

How to you make a glow worm happy?
Cut off its tail and it's delighted.

What do you get if you cross a bee with a bell?
A humdinger.

Why does Piglet smell?
Because he plays with Pooh.

What did Batman say to Robin before they got in the Batmobile?
"Get in the Batmobile, Robin."

What is the biggest insect in the world?
An elephant.

Past, present and future walked into a bar.
It was tense.

Little Jack Horner
Sat in the corner
Eating his Christmas pie.
He stuck in his thumb
And pulled out a plumb
And said: "Hey! This is meant to be steak and kidney."

"Doctor, Doctor, everyone says you are a vampire."
"Necks please."

What do you call a man with a seagull on his head?
Cliff.

How do you catch a bra?
With a booby trap.

How many punks does it take to change a lightbulb?
Two. One to change it and the other to at the old one.

What did the lemon say to the lime?
"Sour you doing?"

What does a Mexican put under his carpet?
Underlay! Underlay!

BATTY BOOKS (3)

Problem children by Miss Bea Haviour

Robotics by Ann Droid

Run for your life by Major Panic

Rusty bedsprings by I P Nightly

Sci-Fi weapons by Ray Gun

Show jumping by Jim Carner

Small crime scene by Miss Dee Meanor

Sneezing fit by A Choo

Solitude by I Malone

Speed reading by Paige Turner

Taxi driver by Minnie Cab

Leave the building now by Rufus Falling

The dripping tap by Lee King

The inevitable by Sue Nora Layter

The river mouth by S Tury

The stolen chestnut by Nick McOnker

The thirsty diner by Phil McCuppup

The unhappy customer by Mona Lott

The worst weekend of my life by Helen Back

Thunder in the night by Henrietta Bean

Top of the form by Hedda De Classe

Trouble In Lancashire by Igor Blimey

Weightlifting by Buster Gut

Why was the biscuit homesick?
He'd been a wafer too long.

What is a cow's favourite breakfast cereal?
Moosli.

What do you call a group of chess players bragging
about their games in a hotel lobby?
Chess nuts boasting in an open foyer.

Did you hear about the man who stayed up all night to
see where the sun went?
It finally dawned on him.

Waiter! Waiter!
There's a fly in my soup.
Sorry sir, force of habit. The chef used to be a tailor.

Why did the grizzly get fired from his job?
He only did the bear minimum.

Why was the baby black and white bear so spoiled?
Because his parents panda'd to his every whim.

Have you ever hunted bear?
No, but I've been fishing in my swimming trunks.

What do you get if you cross a grizzly bear and a harp?
A bear faced lyre.

Why do beavers have fur coats?
Because they'd look silly in anoraks.

"Doctor, Doctor, I'm worried about my breathing."
"I can put stop to that."

What do you get if you cross a skunk with a bear?
Winnie the Pooh!

Why did Tigger look in the lavatory?
He was looking for Pooh.

What pet lays around the house all day?
A carpet.

What pet is also a vegetable?
The petato.

What is a librarian's favourite pet?
A catalogue.

Why did the lion eat the 1000 Watt light bulb?
He wanted a light lunch.

What do you call a man with no arms or legs
swimming the English Channel?
Clever Dick.

What is an owl's favourite lesson?
Owlgebra.

Knock! Knock!
Who's there?
Wendy.
Wendy who?
Wendy river bends we call it a meander.

What do dogs like to eat for breakfast?
Pooched eggs.

What can go as fast as a race horse?
The jockey.

In 1776, what was the most popular dance in America?
Indepen dance.

An asp in the grass
Is a snake,
But a grasp in the ass
Is a goose.

What is worse than raining cats and dogs?
Hailing a taxi.

Why was the lion's neck all wet?
He had a leaky water mane.

How does a farmer count his cattle?
With a cowculator.

What do you get when you cross a skunk with a
boomerang?
A smell you can't get rid of.

"Doctor, Doctor, I feel like a carrot."
"Don't get yourself in a stew."

Which side of a dog has the most hair?
The outside.

Why don't turkeys get invited to dinner parties?
Because they use fowl language.

There are ten kinds of people in this world.
Those who get binary and those who don't.

What do you call a man with a lavatory on his head?
Lou.

What do you call a woman with two lavatories on her head?
Lulu.

What animal drops from the clouds?
Reindeer.

What has four legs and goes 'Boo'?
A cow with a cold.

What do you get if you cross an owl with a skunk?
A bird that stinks, but doesn't give a hoot.

How can you tell if it is a baby snake?
It has a rattle.

Did you hear about the restaurant on the moon?
There was no atmosphere.

What do frogs do with paper?
Rip-it.

He often broke into a song because he couldn't find the
key.

What do you get if you cross a frog and a dog?
A croaker spaniel.

Knock! Knock!
Who's there?
Xavier.
Xavier who?
Xavier your breath and let me in.

Waiter! Waiter!
There's a flea in my soup!
Don't worry, sir, I'll tell him to hop it.

What has three wheels and roars along the bottom of a
lake?
A motor pike and side carp.

What does an eagle write with?
A bald-point pen.

I say, I say, I say.
My wife's just gone on a singing tour to Korea.
Seoul?
No, mainly choral.

What do John Wayne and a map key have in common?
Both are legends.

What do you get if you cross Bambi with a ghost?
Bamboo.

What do you call pretend spaghetti?
Impasta.

What did the queen bee say to the nosy neighbour?
Mind your own bees' nest.

Confucius say he who eat prunes sit on toilet many
moons.

What kind of Mexican food can give you frostbite?
A brrr-ito!

Why did the Mexican chuck his wife over the cliff?
Tequila.

What dis the Mexican fireman call his two sons?
José and Hose B.

Knock! Knock!
Who's there?
Maya.
Maya who?
Maya have a drink of water, please?

Do you file your nails?
No, I throw them away.

"Doctor, Doctor, I have a cricket ball up in my bum."
"Owzat?"

Why was Camelot so famous?
It had terrific knight life.

What is the difference between a butcher and an
insomniac?
One weighs a steak and the other stays awake.

Why did the boy throw the butter out the window?
He wanted to see a butterfly.

Knock! Knock!
Who's there?
Wenceslas.
Wenceslas who?
Wenceslas train home.

What do you call a small tree?
Infantree.

What is the difference between roast beef and pea
soup?
Anyone can roast beef.

What is bright orange and sounds like a parrot?
A carrot.

How many real men does it take to change a lightbulb?
None. They're not afraid of the dark.

How do lizards find their way about?
Gecko location.

Why did the Cyclops close his school?
He only had one pupil.

What do you get if you cross a bag of chips with a
lawnmower?
Shredded treat.

What do you get if you cross a budgerigar with a
lawnmower?
Shredded tweet.

Did you hear about the theatrical performance about
puns?
It was a play on words.

What is worse than seeing a shark's fin?
Seeing his tonsils.

What do trees wear when they go the pool?
Swimming trunks.

Why don't French people eat more than one egg?
Because an egg is an oeuf.

"Doctor, Doctor, I keep breaking wind but it's not smelly."
"You'll need an operation I'm afraid."
"On my bum?"
"No. On your nose."

Did you hear about the shark who ate a bunch of keys?
It got lock jaw.

What do you call a tramp with no legs?
A low down bum.

What do you get if you cross an adult with a moan?
A groan-up.

What did the magician say when he pulled a skewer of meat from his hat?
"Abra-kebabra!"

A man walks into a barber shop and asks: "Bob Dix in here?"
To which the barber replies: "No sir, we just cut hair."

Whey to old records go to die?
Their vinyl resting place.

Last night I dreamed that I was weightless.
I was like, OMg.

Which Victorian terrorised the East End of London by taking his clothes off?
Jack the stripper.

Did you hear about the man who wanted to play water polo?
His horse drowned.

Knock! Knock!
Who's there?
Wayne.
Wayne who?
Wayne are you going to let me in?

Who sings blue Christmas and makes toy guitars?
Elfis.

What is smarter than a talking parrot?
A spelling bee.

What is pink and stands in the corner?
A naughty pig.

What is the fastest vegetable?
A runner been.

Batman doesn't make New Year's Resolutions.
He enforces them.

How can you tell when a snail is lying?
When they say they are not at home.

What is small, red and whispers?
A hoarse radish.

Did you hear the joke about a rope?
OK, I'll skip it.

What does Batman put in his drinks?
Just ice.

What does a polar bear have for tea?
Ice berg-ers.

Why don't grapes get lonely?
Because they hang out in bunches?

Two parrots were on a perch when one says to the
other: "Can you smell fish?"

Doctor: "Go to Brighton, it's great for flu."
Patient: "That's where I went and that's why I've got
it?"

Why is B the hottest letter in the alphabet?
Because it makes oil boil.

Why is H the most exciting letter?
Because it's the start of every holiday.

What do you call a giraffe at the north pole?
Lost.

Have you heard about American knickers?
One yank and they're down.

"I moustache you a question."
"Shave it for later."

What did the general say to his men before they got into their tanks?
"Men, get in your tanks."

Which flowers talk the most?
Tulips.

Why do bananas wear sun cream?
They to stop them peeling.

Doctor: "I have got some good news and some bad news."
Patient: "Give me the good news, first."
Doctor: "I've thoroughly inspected your bottom and it looks OK."
Patient: "What's the bad news?"
Doctor: "I am not a doctor."

Why did the chicken cross the playground?
To get to the other slide.

What is invisible and smells of worms?
A bird burp.

Did you hear about the prawn at the undersea disco?
He pulled a mussel.

Doctor: "You have water on the brain."
Patient: "Is there a cure?"
Doctor: "Yes. A tap on the head.

What do you call a young army?
Infantry.

How much does a pirate pay for an earring?
A Buccaneer.

Julius Caesar walked into a pub and a centurion said:
"Hail, Caesar!"
"Thank you," he replied. "Mine's a pint."

What do pirates like to eat?
Barrrrbecued food.

Why have elephants got big ears?
Because Noddy wouldn't pay the ransom.

"Doctor, Doctor, I've swallowed a roll of film."
"Let's see what develops tomorrow."

A man walks into the pub and orders a Wattle Orseby.
"Wattle Orseby?" asks the barman.
"Oh thank you," he replies. "I'll have a pint please."

How much did the pirate captain pay for his hook and
peg?
An arm and a leg.

Waiter! Waiter!
There's a fly in my soup.
Sorry sir, I missed it when I fished the other ones out.

Knock! Knock!
Who's there?
Ya.
Ya who?
Is there a cowboy around here?

A brain walks into a pub and asks for a pint of beer.
The barman says: "I'm not serving you – you are out of
your head already."

How do you make a fruit punch?
Teach it to box.

What did the ghost say to the giant panda?
"Bamboo!"

What do skunks say in church?
Let us spray.

What do you call a man with a flat fish on his head?
Ray.

What do you call a man without a flat fish on his head?
X-Ray.

Why are horse-drawn carriages so rare?
Because horses can't draw.

Did you hear about the man who didn't like his beard
at first?
It grew on him.

I say, I say, I say.
My wife's just been with a friend to Ireland,
Kilkenny?
No, but he did get on her nerves.

Why does a pair of handcuffs make the perfect
souvenir?
Because they are made for two wrists.

What do you call a boy named Lee that no one talks to?
Lone Lee.

What has a head and a tail, but no body?
A coin.

What do ghosts like to eat?
Ghoulash.

First man: "Do you have a match?"
Second man: "Your face to my bottom?"

How many comedians does it take to change a
lightbulb?
Two. One to change it and the other to say "sock it
to me".

Roses are red,
Violets are blue,
I thought I was ugly,
Until I saw you.

Why does Father Christmas have three gardens?
So he can ho ho ho.

Why are ghosts bad liars?
Because you can see through them.

Which dog can jump higher that a building?
All dogs. Buildings can't jump.

A magician was arrested by the police.
It took him three hours to empty his pockets.

Confucius say man with hand in pocket feel cocky

What do vampires sing on New Year's Eve?
Auld Fang Syne.

Knock! Knock!
Who's there?
Watson.
Watson who?
Watson telly tonight?

Why did the farmer call his pig ink?
Because it ran out of the pen.

How much did Father Christmas' sleigh cost?
Nothing, it was on the house.

Why did the vampire brush his teeth?
To stop bat breath.

Where do yetis go to dance?
Snowballs.

What do you get when you cross a skunk with an elephant?
A big stink.

What do you call a singer with a biscuit on his head?
Lionel Rich Tea.

Waiter! Waiter!
There's a fly on my butter.
It's a butterfly, sir.

What kind of motorbike does Father Christmas ride?
A Holly Davidson.

What has four eyes but cannot see?
Mississippi.

Why is a broken drum the best present you can get?
You just can't beat it.

What do you call a woman in the gutter?
Ingrid.

What is black and white and makes a lot of noise?
A zebra with a drum kit.

What is a snake's favourite lesson?
Hissstory.

How do you know if there is an elephant under your bed?
Your nose is touching the ceiling.

A sleepy young schoolboy from Rye
Was baked by mistake in a pie
To his father's disgust
He emerged from the crust
And said, with a yawn: "Where am I?"

What did Father Christmas say to the smoker?
Please don't smoke, it's bad for my elf.

What goes up but never goes down?
Your age.

If a butcher is six feet tall, what does he weigh?
Meat.

What do lions say before eating?
Let us prey.

Why did the stupid dog have a flat nose?
From chasing parked cars.

Why can't Christmas trees sew?
They always drop their needles.

When do ducks wake up?
The quack of dawn.

Knock! Knock!
Who's there?
Yukon.
Yukon who?
Yukon never get bored of geography.

What is easy to get into but hard to get out of?
Trouble.

How many fishermen does it take to change a
lightbulb?
Five. You should have seen how big the lightbulb was.

Where did Rudolph the red-nosed reindeer go to
school?
Nowhere – he was elf-taught.

What hats do snowmen like?
Ice caps.

How do snowmen travel around?
By icicle.

What do you call an alligator in a vest?
An investigator

Who hides in a bakery at Christmas?
A mince spy.

How many letters are in the alphabet?
25. There's noel at Christmas.

What Christmas carol do they sing in the Sahara?
O camel ye faithful.

What do angry mice send to each other at Christmas?
Cross mouse cards.

Why is a horse like a wedding?
They both need a groom.

What do you get if you eat Christmas decorations?
Tinselitis.

Why don't ostriches fly?
They can't fit in the cockpit.

What do you call a man with a two inch willy?
Justin.

What do you call a magistrate without a willy?
Justice Balls.

Why does a rhinoceros have so many wrinkles?
Have you ever tried ironing one?

Why did the grasshopper go to see a doctor?
It was feeling jumpy.

What do you get if you cross a bell with a skunk?
Jingle smells.

Knock! Knock!
Who's there?
Water.
Water who?
Water way to welcome me home.

Waiter! Waiter!
There's a fly in my soup.
Sorry sir, we have run out of turtles.

What do you get if you cross a cat with a fish?
A purrrana.

Where do you find an ocean with no water?
On a map.

Why did the house go to see a doctor?
It had window panes.

Why don't footballers get hot?
Because of all the fans.

What colour do cats like the best?
Purrple.

Who doesn't go to the emergency room after losing a
thumb?
A magician.

Which famous playwright was terrified of Christmas?
Noël Coward.

Waiter! Waiter!
There's a caterpillar in my salad.
Don't worry, sir, there's no extra charge.

What do you call an attractive volcano?
Lava-ble.

Why is it easy to fool vampires?
Because they are suckers.

What did Father Christmas do when he went speed
dating?
He pulled a cracker.

What does a pilot have to do before landing?
Take off.

How did Mary and Joseph know how heavy the baby
Jesus was?
They had a weigh in a manger.

Confucius say dirty hands make nose itch.

What do you use when your uncle's wife hurts herself?
Auntiseptic.

If a pink house is made from pink bricks and a yellow
house is made from yellow bricks, what is a green
house made from?
Glass.

What is the hardest thing about a parachute jump?
The ground.

Did you hear about the boy who swallowed some coins?
There's no change yet.

Knock! Knock!
Who's there?
Annie.
Annie who?
Annie body home?

Doctor: "I have got some good news and some bad news."
Patient: "Give me the bad news, first."
Doctor: "We have had to cut off both your legs."
Patient: "What's the good news?"
Doctor: "The man in the next bed is looking to buy a pair of slippers."

Why are snowmen good at skiing races?
There's snow competition.

What are Saturday and Sunday the strongest days?
The rest are weekdays.

How many letters are in the alphabet?
27. There's a double U.

What goes ha ha ha thump?
A man laughing his head off.

What did the big telephone say to the little telephone?
You're too young to be engaged.

What did the cloud say to the sun?
"I am under the weather."

Why did the thief wear blue gloves?
So he wasn't caught red handed.

What do you call a woman with a cat on her head?
Kitty.

The sky was dark, the moon was high
We were alone, just she and I.
Her hair was brown, her eyes were too
I knew just what she wanted to do.
So with my courage I did my best
I placed my hand upon her breast.
I trembled, shook and felt her heart
And, very slowly, spread her legs apart.
I knew she was ready, but I didn't know how
After all – I'd never milked a cow.

Why is it getting harder to buy Advent calendars?
Because their days are numbered.

Waiter! Waiter!
There's a fly in my soup.
That's a cockroach. But there is a fly on your bread roll.

What do skeletons say before they eat?
Bone appetite.

Waiter! Waiter!
These eggs are off?
Don't blame me, sir, I only laid the table.

Why didn't the pirate's phone work?
Because he left it off the hook.

I say, I say, I say.
My wife's just gone to Malawi.
Lilongwe?
Yes. It's about 5,000 miles.

How far can a pirate ship travel?
Fifteen miles to the galleon.

Where did the pirate keep his ship?
In the harrrrbour.

I don't like political jokes.
They tend to get elected.

Where do you find a pirate's chocolate?
There is always a Bounty on their head.

How many civil servants does it take to change a
lightbulb?
None. Their job is to keep ministers in the dark.

What do you get if you cross a pirate with an orange drink?
A squashbuckler.

Knock! Knock!
Who's there?
Alex.
Alex who?
Alex plain later, let's go!

Sooty and Sweep robbed a bank.
Police believe Harry Corbett had a hand in it.

Where do you find a pirate's lavatory?
On the poop deck.

How does a pirate blow his nose?
Into an anchor-chief.

Doctor: "I have got some good news and some bad news."
Patient: "Give me the bad news, first."
Doctor: "The treatment is going to cost you more than I thought."
Patient: "What's the good news?"
Doctor: "I can buy a new Rolls Royce."

What did the pirate Father Christmas say?
Yo ho ho ho.

What is the definition of piratophobia?
The fear of a sunken chest.

Who says sticks and stones may break my bones, but words will never hurt me?
Someone who has never dropped a dictionary on his toe.

What is the most slippery country?
Greece.

Why did the orange stop rolling down the hill?
It ran out of juice.

Which word starts and ends with an E, but only has one letter?
Envelope.

Knock! Knock!
Who's there?
Lucas.
Lucas who?
Lucas if it wasn't you who knocked on the door.

What is at the end of everything?
The letter G.

Which nails do carpenters hate to hit?
Fingernails.

How does a train hear?
Through engineers.

Why is tennis such a loud game?
Because each player raises a racquet.

What are the two things you cannot have for breakfast?
Lunch and dinner.

What did one eye say to the other?
Between you and me, something smells.

Why was Cinderella dropped from the netball team?
She ran away from the ball.

Why did the golfer wear two pairs of trousers?
In case he gets a hole in one.

Knock! Knock!
Who's there?
Alaska.
Alaska who?
Alaska later as I've forgotten where I left her.

Which is the tallest building in the world?
The library, because it has the most stories.

How many aerospace engineers does it take to change
a lightbulb?
None. It doesn't need a rocket scientist.

What do you call the tributaries that flow into the Nile?
Juveniles.

What is the world's longest punctuation mark?
The hundred yard dash.

From which school must you drop to graduate?
Parachute school.

I say, I say, I say.
My wife's gone to Northern Italy.
Genoa?
Of course I do! We've been married for ten years.

Teacher: "Who has had one of my apples?"
Pupil: "I haven't touched one of them."
Teacher: "There were two and now there's only one."
Pupil: "That's the one I haven't touched."

Julius Caesar walks into a pub and says: "A martinus, please, barman."
The barman looks up and says: "Don't you mean martini?"
"Listen," replies Caesar, "if I wanted a double, I'd have asked for it."

What is a myth?
A female moth.

A man walks into a pub and someone says: "Nice suit, sir." He looks around but can't see anyone, but again hears a voice saying "You look good in those shoes, too, sir."
"Is that you saying these things, barman?" he asks.
"No sir," he replies. "It's the peanuts – they are complimentary."

Why are Russian dolls pompous?
Because they're full of themselves.

How do you use a doorbell in Egypt?
Toot and come in.

What did the North Korean say when asked his
homelife?
"I can't complain."

When my wife told me to stop impersonating a
flamingo I had to put my foot down.

Doctor: "I haven't seen you for a while."
Patient: "I've been ill."

What kind of a pig should you avoid at a party?
A wild bore.

Man to his friend: "I haven't slept for three days."
Friend: "Why not?"
Man: "Because that would be too long."

What did the man say when given a universal remote
control?
"This changes everything."

Why do flamingos lift up one leg?
Because if the lifted them both they'd fall over.

How did they find out about the roadside workman
stealing from his job?
They went to his house and all the signs were there.

Don't you think that whiteboards are remarkable.

Confucius say person with two feet firmly on ground
have difficulty putting on trousers.

An old lady in a bank asked a fellow customer to help her check her balance.
So he pushed her over.

What do cannibals do at a wedding?
Toast the happy couple.

Did you hear about the girl engaged to a man with a huge nose?
When they kissed it got in the way so she broke it off.

Knock! Knock!
Who's there?
Adore.
Adore who?
Adore is between us so open up.

Pupil: "Sorry sir, I was lost in thought."
Teacher: "Was it unfamiliar territory?"

"Dyslexia rules KO"
"It's 'OK', silly."
"Anyway, dyexials isn't splet kile that."

What was Postman Pat called after he lost his job?
Pat.

If you use crazy paving does it make your walkway a psychopath?

What is an ig?
An Eskimo's home with no loo.

Man: "I am stuck on this crossword clue: overladen postman."
Friend: "How many letters?"
Man: "Millions."

One cow to another: "I'm worried we might get mad cow disease."
Other cow: "Why would that bother you? We're both squirrels."

How does a dog with no nose smell.
Horrible.

Why are my Granny's teeth like stars?
They come out at night.

My granny's cheeks are like peaches.
Football pitches.

Why did the man go to the second hand shop?
To mend his watch.

Boy to his neighbour: "I have found your budgie."
Neighbour: "But this is a cat."
Boy: "Yes, but the budgie is inside it."

Teacher: "Did you just pick your nose?"
Pupil: "No, sir. I was born with it."

When is a good time to avoid your garden?
When the bulbs are shooting.

What time is it when an elephant sits on your fence?
Time to get a new fence.

What do you call a man with a car on his head?
Jack.

Teacher: "If you had 30p in one pocket and 17p in the other, what would you have?"
Pupil: "Someone else's trousers on."

Knock! Knock!
Who's there?
A herd.
A herd who?
A herd you were having a party.

What happened when the glow worm got trodden on?
It was de-lighted.

What sort of bees live in a graveyard?
Zombees.

What did the snake with a cold do?
She adder viper nose.

Why couldn't the viper viper nose?
Because the adder adder handkerchief.

Why did the ram run off the cliff?
He couldn't make a ewe turn.

Why can't dogs dance?
They have two left feet.

What is the closest thing to silver?
The Lone Ranger's bottom.

Why does a Gdansk postman have the longest route
in the world?
Every day he travels from Pole to Pole.

Patient: "Doctor, Doctor. I can't pronounce my F's, T's
and H's."
Doctor: "Well you can't say fairer than that then."

What is a psychopath?
A place where mad people walk.

I say, I say, I say.
My wife's just gone to Moscow.
Is she Russian?
No. Taking her time.

Why did the electrician knock stop work?
Business was light.

What gets larger the more you take away?
A hole.

If there were ten cats on a wall and one jumped off.
How many would be left?
None. They were all copycats.

Why did the student fail his socialism exam?
Lousy Marx.

What did one horse say to the other horse at night?
"Time to hit the hay."

There are three types of people in the world.
Those who can count and those who can't.

How did the trendy bloke burn his mouth?
He drank his tea before it was cool.

What do you get when you cross a burger with a cheetah?
Fast food.

What did one snowman say to the other snowman?
"Can you smell carrots?"

Doctor: "I have got some good news and some bad news."
Patient: "Give me the bad news, first."
Doctor: "I have confirmed it was your blood at the crime scene."
Patient: "What's the good news?"
Doctor: "Your cholesterol is down on last year."

Did you hear about the forgetful Aborigine?
He forgot he'd thrown his boomerang, but it came back to him.

Where do tadpoles change?
In the croak room.

Knock! Knock!
Who's there?
Arthur.
Arthur who?
Arthur any jobs I can do?

Did you hear about the cannibal who ate his
argumentative neighbour?
He disagreed with him.

Atheism.
A non-prophet organisation.

Who was the Black Prince's father?
Old King Coal.

What did the fishing rod say to the fish?
"Catch you later."

How do you make a jam sandwich?
Take two pieces of bread and jam them together.

How many Spaniards does it take to change a
lightbulb?
Juan.

What did the chemistry teacher say to his unruly class?
"If you are not part of the solution, you are part of the
precipitate."

What did the undertaker die from?
Coffin.

How do you wrap up an orange?
Jaffa tape?

First man: "I just got this watch for my wife."
Second man: "That's an interesting swap."

What did the mind reader say to the other mind reader?
"You're fine. How am I?

How do you get two whales in a mini?
Over the Severn Bridge.

Did you hear about the woman who played the piano
by ear?
She broke her earing.

Why is gravity useful?
It is easier to pick up from the floor than the ceiling.

What is dirty, brown and comes out of Cowes?
The Isle of White ferry.

What is the definition of a cannibal?
A person who goes into a restaurant and orders the
waiter.

What is small, furry and smells like bacon?
A hamster.

Why did the man call his old car Dick Turpin?
Because every time he went on the road he held
people up.

What do you call an American with a lavatory on his head?
John.

Why didn't the hypochondriac go to the Dead Sea?
We was nervous of catching what it died from.

What is the most dangerous kind of vegetation?
An ambush.

Knock! Knock!
Who's there?
Abbott.
Abbott who?
Abbott you don't know who this is?

Doctor: "I have got some good news and some bad news."
Patient: "Give me the bad news, first."
Doctor: "We don't know what it is but you will die from it."
Patient: "What's the good news?"
Doctor: "They are going to name the disease after you."

Why do Chemists like nitrates?
Because they are cheaper than day rates.

What did the dragon say to the knight?
"Not tinned food again."

What do you get when you cross a sheep dog with a rose?
A collie flower.

Roses are red,
But here's something new,
Violets are violet,
They've never been blue.

Where there's a will, there's a relative.

Did you hear about the cannibal who went for an after
dinner stroll?
He passed his brother.

Why did the giraffe rarely apologise?
It took him ages to swallow his pride.

What is another name for a sausage?
Groundhog.

Did you hear about the cross lightbulb?
He was incandescent with rage.

What did the Spanish farmer say to his chickens?
Oh lay!

What do you do when a chicken has toothache?
Pullet.

I say, I say, I say.
My wife's just gone to the Welsh borders.
Wye?
I've no idea.

Waiter: "How did you find your steak, sir?"
Customer: "I lifted a chip and there it was."

Pet shop customer: "I'd like to buy a wasp, please."
Assistant: "I'm sorry, sir, but we don't sell wasps."
Customer: "Well you had one in the window last week."

What is the difference between a buffalo and a bison?
Have you ever tried waging your hands in a buffalo?

How did you kill a circus act?
Go for the juggler.

Two cannibals were eating dinner when one says:
"I don't like your mother."
The other replies: "Well just eat the vegetables, then."

Roses are red,
Violets are blue,
Faces like yours,
Belong in a zoo.

What did the lion call the antelope?
Fast food.

Did you hear about the magician who failed to catch a bullet in his teeth?
That's the last time he'll shoot his mouth off.

Confucius say crowded lift smell different to short person.

Knock! Knock!
Who's there?
Bear.
Bear who?
Bare bum.

There was an old scientist called Wright,
Who could travel faster than light.
He departed one day
In a relative way,
And returned the previous night.

Mary had a little lamb
She fed it castor oil
So everywhere that Mary went
It fertilized the soil.

What do you call a Frenchman wearing sandals?
Filipe Flop.

A potato walks into a pub.
All eyes were on him.

How do you get four elephants in a mini?
Two in the front and two in the back.

How do you get a giraffe in a mini?
There's no room as you already have four elephants in
there.

Did you hear about the man with pedestrian eyes?
They looked both ways before they crossed.

Did you know he also had teeth like the Ten
Commandments?
All broken.

What do you get if you cross a plane with a magician?
A flying sorcerer.

What did the beaver say to the stick?
Nice gnawing you.

What do you get if you cross a centipede with a parrot?
A walkie-talkie

Did you hear about the man who was attached by a
packet of cigarettes?
He still has the cigars to prove it.

What is the definition of geriatric?
A German footballer who scores three goals in a game.

Did you hear about the man who gave up palm
reading?
He didn't see any future in it.

How do you make cheese in Wales?
Caerphilly.

What is the difference between a cat and a comma?
One has paws before the claws and the other has the
clause before the pause.

What do you give an elephant with diarrhoea?
Plenty of room.

SOME SLIGHTLY LONGER JOKES

A panda walks into a pub and orders a pint of beer and a hamburger. After eating, he stands up, pulls out a gun and starts firing randomly around the room before turning to leave.

The barman says: "What on earth do you think are you doing?"

"It's what I do," replies the panda and goes.

Later that night the barman looks up pandas in the encyclopaedia where it gives the description: large black and white mammal, native to China, eats shoots and leaves.

A man goes into a pub and slips on some dog mess. Distressed, he sits down and has a drink until, a little while later, another man comes into the pub and also slips on the same mess. The first man chuckles and says: "I did that."

The second man says: "Well ruddy well clear it up then."

A man asks another man if his dog bites and, when he shakes his head, bends down to stroke it. Instantly the dog snarls and savages the first man's hand.

"I thought you said your dog didn't bite," he complains.

"He doesn't," replied the second man. "That's not my dog."

A man walks into a bar and asks for ten glasses of
single malt scotch. The barman pours them out,
whereupon the man pours the first and last on the
floor.
"Why did you do that?" asks the barman.
"Well," replies the man, "I've learned that the first one
always tastes horrid and the last one makes me sick,
but I want to drink whisky."

Three blokes go into a pub and are talking about back
home. "Back in my local in Glasgow, they give me a
free pint for every four I order," says the first.
"In mine," says the second, "if I order two I get the
third one for free."
"That's nothing," says the third (who is none too bright).
"In my local pub they give you the three drinks for
nothing and then they take you upstairs and you have
sex for free."
"Wow," says the first man, thinking of changing venues
to his local. "And has this really happened to you?"
"Well no, not actually to me," says the third man,
"but it happens all the time to my sister."

A cowboy walks into a bar and orders a whisky,
but on seeing the place empty asks: "Where is
everyone."
"They've gone to see Brown Paper Pete be hanged,"
says the barman.
"What kind of nickname is Brown Paper Pete?" asks
the cowboy.
"Well," says the barman, "It's on account of the fact
that he wears a brown paper hat, brown paper shirt,
brown paper trousers and brown paper shoes."

"How odd," says the cowboy, "and what are they
hanging him for?"
"Rustling," replies the barman.

A duck walks into a pub and asks for some peanuts
and the barman says: "I'm sorry, we don't sell
peanuts," so the duck leaves.
The next day the duck comes back and asks for some
peanuts and the barman says: "I told you yesterday, we
don't sell peanuts," so the duck leaves.
The next day the duck comes in again and asks for
some peanuts and the barman says: "Listen mate,
I have told you twice, we don't sell peanuts," so the
duck leaves.
The next day the duck comes in and for the fourth time
asks for some peanuts and the barman, losing his
temper, yells at the duck: "We don't sell peanuts and
if you come in again I am going to nail you to the
wall." so the duck leaves.
The next day the duck walks in and says: "Do you have
any nails?"
Bemused, the barman replies: "No, this is a pub.
We sell drinks and food."
"OK," says the duck, "I'll have some peanuts please."

A man walks into a pub with a monkey, who, whilst
the man is drinking his pint, goes on the rampage,
grabbing some olives off the bar and eating them, then
it takes some cheese rolls off the counter and eats them,
and finally, it jumps onto the snooker table and eats the
cue ball."
"Your monkey just at our cue ball," says the barman.
"Sorry," says the man. "He can't help himself, he just
eats everything in sight. I'll pay for it all."

A couple of weeks later, the man and his monkey come
back to the pub and the monkey leaped onto the bar
and stuck a cocktail cherry and a peanut up his bum.
He then took them both out and ate them. "Right!"
the barman says to the man. "That is the limit! He just
stuck a cherry and peanut up his bum and then ate
them."
"I know," says the man, wearily. "Since he ate that cue
ball he now measures everything before eating it."

Two men are walking their dogs, a Labrador and a
Chihuahua, and decide to go for a pint, but a sign
outside the pub says that dogs are not allowed in.
The Labrador owner says: "Just follow me and do
what I do."
"I'm sorry gentlemen," says the barman. "No dogs are
allowed in here."
"But he is my guide dog," says the Labrador owner.
"OK," says the barman.
"And so is mine," says the other man.
"Yeah, right!" says the barman to the second man.
"A Chihuahua?"
"They sold me a what?!"

A man walks into a pub and asks the barman if, by
showing him something unbelievable, he can have a
free beer, to which the barman agrees. So the man puts
a hamster and two hens on the bar and the two hens
start to sing: 'There ain't nobody here but us chickens.'
"I've seen many things in my time," says the impressed
barman, "but that is incredible. Here's your pint and
I'll give you £1,000 for the hens – they would be great
for business."

The man agrees but, having completed the transaction, another patron says: "You sold the hens too cheaply."

"Hens are easy to replace," replies the man sipping his beer. "The hamster is a ventriloquist."

A magician's parrot would always ruin his act by saying things like: "the card is up his sleeve," or "he has a rabbit under his hat."

One day, when the magician was working on board a cruise ship, the vessel hit something and sank, and he found himself floating alone on a piece of wood. Shortly afterwards, the parrot landed on it too and for three days just sat there staring at the magician. Eventually the parrot spoke up and said: "OK. You win. What did you do with the ship?"

A man is sitting at a bar, staring at his drink for about half an hour, when a big bully of a biker strides up to him, grabs his drink and gulps it down in one swig. The first man starts crying and says: "This is the worst day of my life. I can't do anything right. I overslept this morning, missed an important meeting and was fired. I went to get my car and found it had been stolen and I realised I had forgotten to renew my insurance. I left my briefcase on the bus and when I got home I found my wife in bed with the gardener and my dog bit me. So I came to this pub to try and work up the courage to put an end to my life and you show up and drink the blooming poison."

Two old friends, Bill and Bob, are sitting at their favourite bar, drinking beer, when Bill sighs and says: "I'm tired of going through life without an education so tomorrow I am going to go to the local college and sign up for some classes."

The next day, Bill goes to the college and is accepted up for the four basic classes, Maths, English, History and Logic. "What exactly is Logic?" he asks.

"Well," says the registrar, "let me give you an example. Do you own any weed killer?"

Bill nods and the registrar says: "Because you own some weed killer, I can deduce that you have a lawn and I can further deduce that you have a house. I can then deduce that you have a family, which leads me to know that you have a wife and therefore logic tells me that you are a heterosexual."

"I am a heterosexual," says Bill. "So Logic gets you all that from whether or not I have some weed killer?"

That night Bill tells Bob about the courses he has signed up for and how excited he is about Logic.

"What's Logic?" asks Bob.

"Well," says Bill, "let me give you an example of how it works. Do you have any weed killer?"

"No," says Bob.

"Then," says Bill triumphantly, "logically, you are a homosexual."

A man takes his Rottweiler dog to the vet and says: "My dog's cross-eyed, is there anything you can do for him, please?"

"Well let's have a look at him, shall we?" replies the vet and he picks up the dog and examines his eyes, checks his teeth. Eventually he says: "I'm going to have to put him down."

"What?" asks the horrified man. "Because he's cross-eyed?"

"No," replies the vet. "Because he's very heavy."

An eighty year-old man went to see his doctor. "Can you help me, please, Doc?" he asks.

"Well that depends on the problem, sir."

"It is this," says the man. "Every morning, regular as clockwork at seven o'clock, I have a bowel movement of considerable magnitude."

"OK," says the doctor. "Well at you age I think that is very healthy. So what is your problem?"

"I don't get up until eight-thirty!"

Jack Hawkins met up with Long John Silver and, looking at his hook, peg leg and eye patch, he asked: "How did you lose your hand, Long John?"

"Arrrr, lad," he replies. "Shark bit it off, arrrr."

"Oh," says Jack. "And how did you lose your leg, Long John?"

"Arrrr, lad," he replies. "Shark bit it off, arrrr."

"Wow," says Jack. "And how did you lose your eye, Long John?"

"Arrrr, lad," he replies. "Seagull plopped in it, arrrr."

"Really?" asks the boy. "I understand the shark bites, but I didn't know you could lose your eye to bird poo, Long John."

"Arrrr, lad," he replies. "You can if you forget you've lost your hand."

Long ago lived a seaman nick-named Captain Braveheart. He fearlessly led his men into battle and fought at the front in each skirmish. One day, having only recently selected a new crew member as his second mate, they spied a pirate ship on the horizon and the crew seemed nervous as he steered them into battle. "Fetch me my red shirt, please second mate," he cried and, donning the item leapt aboard the other ship and led his men to victory.

The next day the look-out spotted two pirate ships on the horizon. And the captain again called for his red shirt and again led his men to victory.

Intrigues by his wardrobe changes, the second mate asked him: "Captain. Why do you change into your red shirt before battle?"

"Well," replied the captain. "It is an old trick I learned as a lad. My red shirt would hide the blood if I were wounded and so no one would know and they would fight on, unafraid."

The next day the look-out spotted a fleet of pirate ships on the horizon and, as they turned as one to fight his single vessel, the captain called out: "Fetch me my brown trousers, please second mate."

The Lone Ranger and Tonto went camping in the desert and both awoke in the middle of the night.

"Kemosabe," says Tonto. "Look up and what do you see?"

"I see millions and millions of stars, Tonto. Why do you ask?" says the Lone Ranger

"And what that tell you?" says Tonto.

The Lone Ranger ponders for a minute then says,

"Astronomically speaking, it tells me there are millions

of galaxies. Time wise, it appears to be approximately a quarter past three in the morning. Theologically, the Lord is all powerful and we are small and insignificant and meteorologically, it seems we will have a beautiful day tomorrow. What does it tell you, Tonto?"

"Kemosabe! Someone stole our tent!"

A rabbit goes into a café and orders a cheese and ham toasted sandwich. Being extremely hungry he gulps it down and immediately asks the waitress to bring him another, but this time with tomato and pickle.

This is also gulped down and once again he calls the waitress over, but this time he orders a baked bean and brown sauce toasted sandwich.

Having dispatched that in a couple of mouthfuls, he then orders three more, a cheese and pickle, a carrot and mayonnaise and one with only strawberry jam in it.

Having wolfed them all down he starts to feel a little unwell and calls the waitress over for a final time.

"Do you have a bathroom please?" he asks.

"Yes, sir, it is over there. Are you feeling OK – you look a little peaky?"

"Actually I'm not feeling well at all."

"What wrong?" she asks.

"Mixing me toasties."

A pirate and his parrot, were adrift in a lifeboat following a dramatic escape from a fierce battle and, while looking through the boat's provisions, the pirate found an old lamp. He rubbed it and suddenly a genie appeared in a puff of smoke. "What is your command,

oh master?" said the genie. "I can grant you one wish
of whatever you heart desires."
The pirate thought for a bit, which was probably
longer than he had ever thought as he was none too
bright, and then he said: "Turn the sea into rum, please
genie."
In an instant, the waters all around were turned into
golden rum and the genie vanished. The parrot
looked at the pirate and said: "I can't believe it.
You are such an idiot. Now we'll have to pee in the
boat."

A man walked into a pub in Glasgow with a giraffe
and ordered twenty five pints. While he drank one of
them the giraffe necked the other 24 and promptly
passed out on the floor. As the man was leaving the
barman pointed to the animal sprawled across his
floor and said "Hey - you'll no be leaving that lyin'
there?
To which the man replied: "That's no' a lion, that's a
giraffe."

Two friends were walking home late one night and one
of them decides to take a shortcut through the
graveyard and heard a very strange sound, like music
being played backwards.
The next night the two of them went into the graveyard
to listen and see if there was something going on or f he
was just imagining things, but, sure enough, they hear
the same strange music.
The next night they went again to the graveyard armed
with a tape recorder to catch the sound and listen to it
in daylight when it wasn't so scary.

The next morning the two friends met up and one says – I know what it is. I played the tape backwards and listen – it is the Moonlight Sonata."

Perplexed, they went straight to the graveyard and started looking for where they thought the sound came from when one of them shouts, "I know what is going on. Look, this is the grave of Ludwig van Beethoven." But why is his ghostly music playing backwards?" asks the other.

"It's simple. He's decomposing."

A man bought a parrot from the pet shop, but when he got home the bird unleashed a loud torrent of abuse, using every swear word under the sun. The man was very taken aback and covered the cage and the bird went quiet. But every time he lifted the cloth, the bird carried on where he left off.

Eventually the man could take in no longer, but neither could he take it back as he was too embarrassed, so he stuffed it into his freezer. After half an hour he was filled with remorse and opened the door to find the parrot still alive but apologising profusely for his language. "I promise I won't ever swear again, I am so very sorry for my behaviour," it said. "Oh, and by the way, what did the chicken do?"

A drunk finds an old lamp and gives it a rub. A genie appears in a puff of smoke and says: "I am the genie of the lamp oh great master and I will grant you three wishes."

"Marvellous," says the drunk. "I'd like a glass of whisky that never empties, please." In another puff of smoke, a tumbler filled with the most exquisitely blended scotch appears on the table and the drunk reaches for it. He raises the glass to his lips and starts drinking the malt and it just keeps flowing.

After half an hour, the genie interrupts him with a polite cough. "Er, master?" he says. "What would you like for your other two wishes?"

Slightly the worse for wear now, the drunk looks at the genie over the rim of his glass and slurs: "I'll like two more of these please."

The Lone Ranger and Tonto were out riding when the Lone Ranger had to answer the call of nature. While squatting behind a bush a snake reared up and bit him on his undercarriage.

In a panic and frozen with fear he told Tonto to get to town and ask the doctor what to do, so off he went.

In town the doctor had clear advice for Tonto: "Take a knife and make an x on the spot where he was bitten and then suck out all of the poison."

Arriving back at the now distraught Lone Ranger, Tonto says: "The doctor says you're going to die."

Once upon a time, a cabbage and a turnip were walking down the street, when a car drove up on the curb and squashed the cabbage. The turnip called for help and did the best he could to save his friend as he was rushed into the operating theatre. After several hours the doctor came out and said: "I have some good news and I have some bad news for you."

"Please tell me the good news first," said the turnip.
"Well the good news is that he's alive."
"And what's the bad news?" asked the turnip.
"He'll be a vegetable for the rest of his life."

A policeman stopped a driver who appeared to have a baby bear in the front seat and, on rolling down the window, his suspicions were confirmed. "What on earth are you doing with that bear?" he exclaimed. "You should take it to the zoo immediately."
The next week the policeman saw the same driver and, yet again, he had the baby bear in his passenger seat, so he flagged him down.
"I thought you said you were going to take that bear to the zoo?"
"I did," said the man. "He enjoyed it so much that this weekend we are going to go to the seaside."

A woman boarded a bus with her baby and a driver says: "Do you know that is the ugliest baby I have ever seen in my life."
Bursting into tears she sat down at the back of the bus next to a kindly old gentleman. "What on earth is the matter?" he asked.
"The bus driver just insulted me," she sobbed.
"Well you can't let him get away with it," says the gent. "You go back to him and stand up for yourself while I look after your monkey."

Two Legionnaires had been wandering in the desert for days without food or water, when they spied bustling market at an oasis. Realising it wasn't a mirage they rushed up to the first stall and cried: "Smallholder, we have been travelling in the desert for many days and dehydrated. We shall surely die soon unless you have some water you can sell us - tell us, do you have any, please?"

The smallholder shook his head and replied "I'm sorry, but all I have to sell is bowls full of jelly, topped with custard and cream, and lovingly sprinkled with hundreds and thousands."

The legionnaires look at each other, mildly surprised, and move on to the next stall, where they ask the smallholder, "Mr purveyor of fine foodstuffs and the like, we have been travelling through the desert for days, deprived of the necessary beverages and foodstuffs which are required for survival. We shall surely die soon, unless you can sell us some skins of water, please."

The smallholder looked at them a little embarrassed. "Gentlemen, tragic as I admit it is, I have none of the ingredients necessary to life for which you ask me. All I have to sell is this large bowl of jelly topped with custard and cream and sprinkled with hundreds and thousands, with a little cocktail cherry in the middle at the top – see?" he said, pointing out the glacé cherry. "I cannot help you."

The legionnaires looked at each other in desperation and ran to the next stall, where they demanded of the smallholder, "Please. We need water or we'll die. We've been travelling without liquid for days and need some now. Do you have any you can sell us?"

The smallholder looked at his curl-ended shoes in shame as he confessed: "I am so sorry, but all I have to sell you is a bowl of jelly, with custard, cream and hundreds and thousands. I can't help you. I'll have to condemn you to a long and lingering death through dehydration."

The legionnaires were really worried by this point, and they went through the market, stall by stall, asking each smallholder whether they had any water they could sell them, and thus save their lives, but each smallholder gave the same reply. All that was on offer were bowls of jelly with cream, custard and hundreds and thousands.

Dejected and resigned to their grim fate, the legionnaires left the desert market and walked off into the setting sun more parched than ever. As they did so, one turned and said: "That was really odd – a big market in the middle of nowhere and all they sold was bowls of jelly with custard, cream and hundreds and thousands."

"I know," replied the other. "It was a trifle bazaar."

A SMALL SELECTION
OF SILLY ANAGRAMS

A decimal point — I'm a dot in place

A gentleman — Elegant man

An Intel Pentium Processor — Customer nipple not arisen

Astronomers — No more stars

Benson and Hedges — NHS been a godsend

Boddingtons, the cream of Manchester — Boddington's stomach ache fermenter

Clint Eastwood — Old west action

Conversation — Voices rant on

Debit card — Bad credit

Dormitory — Dirty room

Eleven plus two — Twelve plus one

Funeral — Real fun

Hot water — Worth tea

Motorway Service Station — I eat coronary vomit stews

Mummy — My mum

Performance related pay — Mere end of year claptrap

Schoolmaster — The classroom

Stella Artois, reassuringly expensive — Pint o' lager virtually erases sexiness

The country side	- No city dust here
The Detectives	- Detect thieves
The eyes	- They see
The Houses of Parliament	- Loonies far up the Thames
Vacation time	- I am not active

About the author

Following a peripatetic childhood ambling amiably between three boarding schools and seven different family homes, Julian got the travel bug early and has maintained an enthusiasm for it despite masking an adventurous life with a more conventional desk career in public relations.

When not office bound he has managed to travel off the beaten track through jungles, remote seas, swamps, mountains and veld. He has maintained his sense of humour despite having been arrested, mugged, shot at, charged by wild animals, got himself spectacularly lost in the desert (so is not always the luckiest travel companion) and developed a taste for dry martini cocktails.

More by accident than design he has accumulated a wealth of experiences engaging with nomadic tribes, smugglers and wild animals of all imaginable shape and size, while still finding time to donate blood to both the UK NHS and rather too many mosquitoes.

In addition to his communications activities, Julian is author of The Cape Crusaders – about his experiences driving a Dennis fire engine from the northern-most tip of Europe to the southern-most point in Africa – and is Chair of a small philanthropic fund designed to empower and develop young people's true potential.

The Book of Cringe is his first collection of old jokes.

Lightning Source UK Ltd.
Milton Keynes UK
UKOW04f0046121215

264581UK00001B/27/P